BRITAIN
A WORLD BY ITSELF

BRITAIN

A WORLD BY ITSELF

Reflections on the landscape by eminent British writers

WITH COMMENTARIES BY DR FRANKLYN PERRING

Photographs by Paul Wakefield

LITTLE, BROWN & COMPANY

BOSTON   TORONTO

Library of Congress Catalog Card No. 84-81453

First American edition

Published by arrangement with Aurum Press Limited, London

Published simultaneously in Canada
by Little, Brown & Company (Canada) Limited

Printed in Italy

CONTENTS

A DEVON RIVER
TED HUGHES 10

THE CHESIL BANK
JOHN FOWLES 18

THE WILTSHIRE DOWNS
GEOFFREY GRIGSON 32

CHICHESTER HARBOUR
RICHARD WILLIAMSON 44

A SUFFOLK VALLEY WOOD
RONALD BLYTHE 54

THE FENS
EDWARD STOREY 64

THE BLACK MOUNTAINS
JAN MORRIS 76

A THICKET IN LLEYN
R. S. THOMAS 92

THE LAKES
MELVYN BRAGG 104

THE HIGHLANDS
IAIN CRICHTON SMITH 126

ORKNEY
GEORGE MACKAY BROWN 140

THE CONTRIBUTORS

RONALD BLYTHE, poet, novelist, essayist and critic, is perhaps best known as the author of *Akenfield,* a classic portrait of village life in East Anglia, where he himself lives and writes.

MELVYN BRAGG, writer and broadcaster, is Head of Arts at London Weekend Television and editor and presenter of the South Bank Show. Several of his novels are set in the Lake District, about which he has also written in *Land of the Lakes.* Now living in London, he escapes to his native Cumbria as often as he can.

GEORGE MACKAY BROWN's writing has its centre in images and themes from Orkney, where he has always lived. His most recent novel, *Time in a Red Coat,* is about war and man's chances of survival. He is currently preparing new books of poems and a book of long stories.

JOHN FOWLES achieved worldwide acclaim for his second novel, *The French Lieutenant's Woman,* published in 1969, and since then has consolidated his reputation with *The Ebony Tower* and *Daniel Martin.* In 1979 he wrote the text for *The Tree,* published by Aurum Press. He lives in Dorset.

GEOFFREY GRIGSON is a well-known poet, literary critic and anthologist. His lifelong interest in the countryside is reflected in his writings, and his compilations include many books on the English landscape. Born in Cornwall, he now lives in Wiltshire.

TED HUGHES has published many collections of poetry, among them *Moortown,* a verse journal of his experiences of farming in Devon, where he lives.

JAN MORRIS, who is half Welsh, has a home in the Black Mountains. Historian as well as travel-writer, she collaborated with Paul Wakefield on the picture essay *Wales: The First Place,* and in 1984 Oxford University Press published her major study of the country, *The Matter of Wales.*

FRANKLYN PERRING has been General Secretary of the Royal Society for Nature Conservation since 1979. In that capacity he writes regularly on conservation issues in *Natural World,* the RSNC magazine. He is co-author of the *Atlas of the British Flora* and has written or edited ten other botanical books.

IAIN CRICHTON SMITH is described in *The Penguin Book of Scottish Verse* as 'the best Scottish poet now writing in English'. Born on the island of Lewis, he now lives and writes in Taynuilt, Argyll.

EDWARD STOREY was born in the Isle of Ely, Cambridgeshire. He has made a particular study of the Fen country, about which he has written four books, and is the author of *A Right to Song: A Life of John Clare.* He is also a poet, librettist and regular broadcaster on radio and television.

R. S. THOMAS is a native of Wales and was vicar of the parish in which he now lives. He has published a dozen collections of poetry for which he has won various awards, including the Queen's Gold Medal for Poetry in 1964. His latest collection of poems, *Between Here and Now,* was published in 1981.

RICHARD WILLIAMSON, son of Henry Williamson, is, like his father, passionately involved with natural history. Author of numerous wildlife articles, he has also written three books, one an account of Kingley Vale, the oldest yew forest in Europe, of which he is warden. With his wife Anne he is currently preparing the definitive biography of his father.

A
DEVON RIVER

TED HUGHES

Nymet

No map or Latin ever

Netted one deity from this river.
TAW meant simply *water*.
What were her true names
When she poured these pools from her ewer

And gave her breast to the strange hunters
Who followed the dying Mastodon
That came down through Belstone?
How did they name her

When she drew their offerings and prayer
Into her tunnel water
With the brother-blood of heron and otter
As into cave-womb rock?

THE RIVER TAW AT SKAIGH WARREN, DEVON

THE RIVER TAW NEAR ROWDEN MOOR

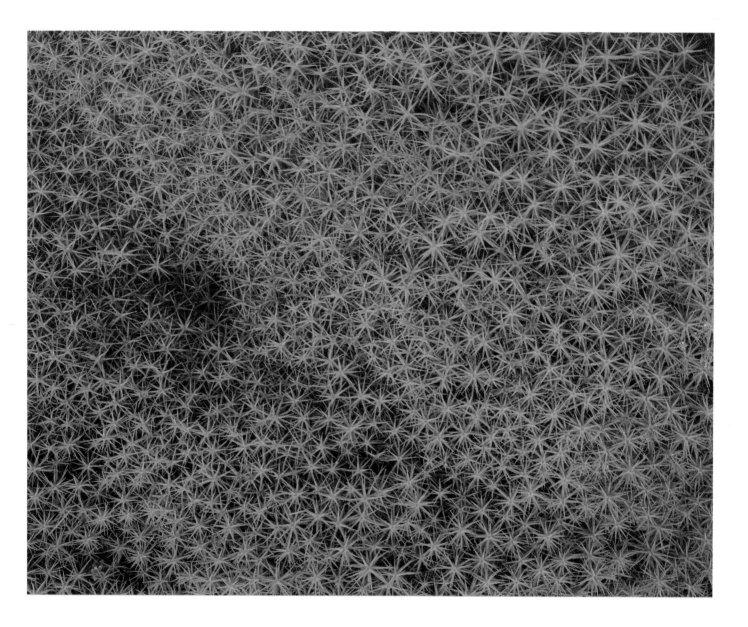

Then with yellow smoky nettle pollen
And the first thorn's confetti
Crushed the May bridegroom's
Head into her flood?

Afterwards, she bore him, without fail,
All summer a splendour
Of eel-wreaths and a glut of white peal,
And right on through summer and winter the glow-cold

Sea-new salmon. Her names and her coombes
Deepened together: 'Our Bride, Our Mother, Our Nurse'.
Where is she now?
A fairy

Drowned in the radio-active Irish Sea.
Blood-donor
To the South-West Water Authority.
Her womb's been requisitioned

For the cloacal flux, the privy curse
Of the Express Dairy Cheese Factory –
'Biggest in Europe'.
A miasma

Mourns on the town bridge, at odd hours,
Over her old home, now her grave.
That's her.
She rots

But still stirs – a nightly, dewy spectre,
Nameless revenant
In her grave-clothes, resurrected
By her maternal despair

For her dying fish. She wipes their lips
Of the stuff that weeps
From her curdled dug since it became
The fistula of a thousand farms. That's her –

The milk-herd's daily discharge of detergent,
The sheep-flock's and the beef-herd's purgation,
Ferment of silage in her every vein,
The earthen town's overkill of hygiene –

And so we have christened her: Sewer of all Sewers.

But she is that Celtic apparition,
The fatal vision, who comes near the end of stories:
The Washer at the Ford.
The death-rags that she washes and washes are ours.

During the last forty years the Water Authorities have ravaged Britain's rivers in their quest for greater flood control. Thousands of miles of streams and rivers have been dredged and bankside herbs, shrubs and trees removed, turning winding wildernesses into straight, dull, sterile aqueducts in which no wildlife can survive. Simultaneously the increased drainage has led adjacent farmers to plough up old meadows, removing hedges and copses. In the process whole landscapes have been destroyed, and some of our most loved wild creatures have been lost from large areas of the countryside. Herons which once nested in the copses and fed on frogs in marshy river margins have gone from many valleys, while the shy otter, which until the mid-1950s was common along overgrown streams and shaded river banks in every county of Britain, is now absent from almost the whole of England and Wales.

The initial decline of the otter was almost certainly due to organochlorine pesticides, particularly dieldrin, the use of which at the end of the 1950s began contaminating waterways and the fish upon which the otters depended. But their failure to recover when dieldrin was banned was due to the fact that in the 1960s and 1970s most of their habitats had been disturbed or destroyed.

In 1981 the Wildlife and Countryside Act imposed on Water Authorities the duty to further the conservation of the flora and fauna so far as this is consistent with their prime duty of flood control and land drainage. Yet the destruction still continues.

Otters and other water-dependent creatures will only survive in Britain if they are given priority on some water courses. Does every stream and river have to be canalized? And even on those where work is essential, cannot secluded stretches be left untouched or one bank remain uncleared? From these refuges the habitat could be recolonized, after the drag-line has passed, by native plants and animals.

There are encouraging signs that this is beginning to happen: Severn-Trent Water Authority has left riverside trees and persuaded farmers to manage them as sources of timber or firewood so that falling branches do not impede the water flow; the South West, on one of its rivers, has created a small marshy area and cut off a meander to leave a wooded islet suitable for otter cover. But is this too little, too late, to repair the havoc already created?

The Wildlife and Countryside Act is a challenge to Water Authorities: from now on they must all take a responsible and constructive attitude to nature conservation and carry out their duties in such a way that they create as many habitats as they destroy, leaving the countryside they move through as rich or richer in wildlife than before they came. They must also appreciate that their work should serve the whole community and not just the landowners, who for several decades have used political pressure to put through drainage schemes – largely paid for from the public purse – thereby increasing the value of the land for their private gain while depriving the public of a priceless landscape.

THE RIVER TAW AT BELSTONE CLEAVE

THE CHESIL BANK

JOHN FOWLES

I seldom go to the Chesil Bank without feeling faintly frustrated. Was ever a landscape so ridiculously narrow and long, so determined to thwart the visitor? It looks a nonsense on maps: a primitive long-handled stone axe or knobkerrie, the head formed by the Portland peninsula – the only thing to which, until quite recently, its southern end was connected.

Walking the Chesil is for masochists only. Half a mile on the shingle is worse than two miles on solid land. Understanding it – that is, trying to plough through the endless shifting pebbles of professional geographical and geological theory as to why it behaves as it does, indeed why it exists at all, is almost as arduous, at least to the poor layman. This most strandlike of strands breaks all the rules. Everywhere else in the Channel, beach material is carried eastward; here it is westward, and lightest furthest. Its smallest shingle goes to the north-west, its largest to the south-east, and with such obsessive exactitude that an old Chesil hand, landing in a thick fog on any of its eighteen miles, knows just where he is by pebble size. But there it is, one of the great wonders of English landscape, a flagrant anomaly in that of generally cliffed Dorset. The old notion that it all blew up in one night can sometimes seem the most plausible.

THE CHESIL BANK, DORSET, LOOKING WEST

THE CHESIL, LOOKING EAST

The sharp shelves of the beach, its undertow and rogue waves, mean that only fools ignore the warnings against swimming. The nearest lifeboat, at Lyme Regis, has almost every year to make the twelve or fifteen mile journey to the Bank; another swimmer has learnt the hard way – only too often, the final way. The onshore beach anglers are wiser, and far more picturesque, in their scattered groups, with their long rods and even longer vigils for the bass and other fish they are after.

The Chesil is rich in an older human history. This was once a distinctly lawless area; and all its villages, Burton Bradstock, Swyre, Puncknowle, Abbotsbury, Langton Herring, East Fleet and Chickerell, were guilty. An eighteenth-century traveller said that all the inhabitants of Abbotsbury, 'including the Vicar', were smugglers, thieves and wreck-plunderers. They evolved also a special form of fishing, seine-netting, and a special double-ended fishing-boat, the lerret. Nets were rowed round shoals of fish such as mackerel and sprats and then hauled in by teams on shore. At Burton the old cry of 'Vish strayen!' (fish straying into inshore shoals) or the sound of the mackerel horn would at once bring normal life to an abrupt stop, as everyone flocked to the beach. These fishermen were highly superstitious. They never shot a seine on Sundays, or harmed a seagull (for these held drowned sailors' souls). Their lerrets always carried a holed (or holy) stone at bow and stern for luck; if this failed, and the boat was bewitched, a dead mackerel was stuck with pins and brought aboard. Holed stones were used by the smugglers also, as sinking-weights on their tubs of brandy.

For nearly half its eighteen-mile length, the Chesil runs side by side with an inland lagoon, the Fleet, which varies in width from half a mile to a long stone's throw, a mere hundred yards. It has only one narrow outlet to the sea, and so is very shallow; halfheartedly tidal, with flats of rich organic silt, its western end more brackish than fully salt. This makes it a great haven and larder for aquatic birds. Much of its inner shore can be walked. The sheltered backslope of the Chesil opposite has low vegetation, salt-tolerant plants that find a living there. Its eastern half is not quite deserted; here and there you may see ramshackle huts made of driftwood, like fragments from a set for *Peter*

Grimes. The western end is lonelier, for it is one of the oldest bird sanctuaries in Britain; its famous swannery goes back to medieval times. The mute swans there breed colonially, in the charge of a swanherd, and are much less aggressive than the solitary-nesting pairs of the normal river bank.

I was beside the Fleet at Herbury at the end of April, watching migrating parties of bar-tailed godwit, the males in their rich rust-red breeding plumage, come in over the Chesil and land to wash and feed. Some early terns also; grey and ringed plover, dunlin, a turnstone, oystercatchers, shelduck, a small flock of red-breasted merganser, swimming in their strange flattened way, like would-be torpedoes, after the flounders and eels they feed on here. Finally I heard one of the loneliest and most haunting of all bird cries. Whimbrel; seven came in, and landed beside the godwits. It was a very calm evening, and I watched this beautiful assemblage in the pooled reflection of a greeny-yellow field of rape inland across the water.

Not all bird-watching experiences at the Fleet are quite so classical. A few weeks earlier I was watching two swans fly in to land on a meadow, where sheep grazed. Then suddenly a quite ridiculous flash of shocking pink also flew into my field of vision. It landed some fifty yards from where the swans were, then minced delicately across the grass to them for all the world like some effete ponce coming to make a proposition. The Fleet evidently has three-star rating for *Phoenicopterus ruber,* as they are quite often seen there when they escape. A wild South American flamingo in an English sheep-meadow belongs much more to Lewis Carroll than ornithology.

Abbotsbury is the undisputed queen of the Chesil: one of the most beautiful villages in west Dorset, saved from having become a popular seaside resort by the Chesil itself, or its danger as a bathing place. One's first view, coming high from the west, of the lyncheted hill crowned by St Catherine's Chapel, with the Fleet and the Chesil stretching vastly away beyond, is one of the most beautiful in England. I have seen it in many different lights and moods. It is always fresh, verdant, acutely pleasing; a slightly fairy-tale domain spread at one's feet. The 600-foot chalk downs that overlook the Chesil are dense with the tumuli, lynchets, trackways, stone circles and enclosures of earlier

THE FLEET AND CHESIL BANK FROM WEARS HILL

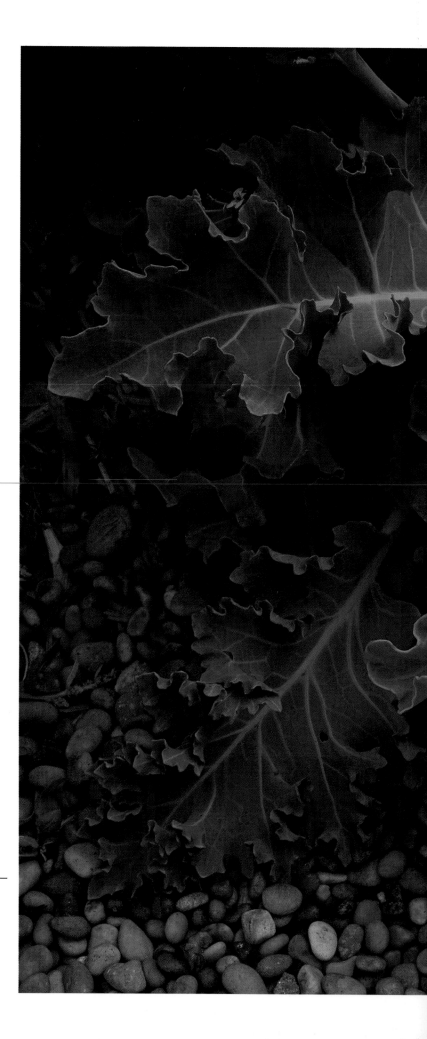

SEAKALE ON THE CHESIL

mankind. This steep green backdrop is an essential part of the magic by the sea below.

Abbotsbury can satisfy the botanist and gardener, too. Its Subtropical Gardens, in a wood only a few hundred yards behind the Bank, grow many very rare plants and trees. Founded by the first Countess of Ilchester in 1765, a little way back from her now ruined summer villa directly above the Chesil, the gardens lie within the vital belt of warmer winter temperature afforded by the sea, where frosts are very rare. That is why such splendid palm trees and camellias and magnolias survive there. The most famous is a huge *Magnolia campbellii,* now sixty foot tall, and a breathtaking sight with its enormous pink tulip-flowers in full bloom – almost as unreal, or surreal, as the flamingo.

From the Subtropical Gardens you have only to stroll a short distance to see a very different flora – that of the backslope of the Chesil Bank itself. Many rare native plants such as the sea pea and sea kale, the yellow horned-poppy and shrubby sea-blite, survive this difficult environment. One of the most charming – and commonest – is the scurvy-grass, *Cochlearia danica.* Its myriad tiny flowers mist the bare shingle with an ethereal lilac-tinged ashy light in spring. Closer to, you must kneel; they are like alpine plants. Here as elsewhere the Chesil is lined at the back with groves of tamarisk. Nearby grows another 'foreigner', the Duke of Argyll's tea-plant, a favourite shrub of mine because of the colour of its newly opened flowers. One *Hortus* I have describes *Lycium chinense* as 'dull lilac purple'; which deserves a suit for libel.

Its presence is apt, because the aesthetic essence, the deepest appeal of the Chesil Bank is to me oriental. It calls to that ancient Chinese delight in nature and landscape, to that metaphysical respect for the simple we associate with Zen Buddhism. It is above all an elemental place, made of sea, shingle and sky, its dominant sound always that of waves on moving stone; from the great surf and pounding 'ground seas' of sou'westers, to the delicate laps and back-gurglings of the rare dead calms. That zone between the dry, bleached pebbles above the waves and the wetted ones within their reach, where their colours come alive – 'where they flower', as an old fisherman once put it to me – can become hypnotic. One walks with head bowed, oblivious to all but that constantly rewashed world at one's feet. Most of the pebbles are of

Cretaceous chert and flint, but pebbles of much more ancient stones from Devon, even Cornwall, appear. However, the Chesil was always a ferocious trapper of sailing-ships, and countless of them carried stone as ballast; modern geologists treat exotic 'erratics' here with caution. The beach has airier beauties; a phenomenon I have seen once or twice in misty conditions is the Chesil in the sky, a kind of aerial glow that continues long after the actual strand disappears from view. By an exquisite illusion it becomes a dim golden ghost or halo over its vanished real self below.

I can see the Chesil from where I live, but I do not feel attached to it in a literary way; it is not 'my' country, fond though I am of it. As with all special landscapes nowadays, celebrating it in old-fashioned terms raises ethical problems. If the Chesil and the Fleet and their hinterland need anything, it is practical preserving and guarding, not descriptive prose. They are in any case their own prose – and poetry – and in a language infinitely more subtle and rich than words. Celebration entails a certain blindness, a seeing only the good side; what mercifully remains, not what encroaches and threatens. I have not mentioned the seeping of Weymouth north-westwards, nor the increasing 'leisure use' of the East Fleet. I have not mentioned that Herbury, where I watched the birds, is also a proposed nuclear power station site – on the shelf at the moment, but not certainly dropped for ever. I have not mentioned the commonest (in both senses) sign of life on the backslope of the Bank – the foul scatter of plastic rubbish, blown over from where it washes up after being thrown overboard by Channel shipping; nor a grim reality of the green downs that overlook the Fleet and Chesil. These days they are endless 'improved' grassland, almost all their wild flowers gone. The great sarsen stones of the Neolithic long-barrow in the hills behind Abbotsbury, the Grey Mare and her Colts, are only too fittingly funereal: they stand among ecologically dead fields.

So I cannot *only* celebrate the Chesil. If I acted in its best interest, I suspect I should say it is not worth the visit. But alas, it is. All I can pray for is what I am myself, the loving visitor; and the good sense and decency in human affairs that remains as thin – and sometimes as improbable – a barrier against our worse and greedier selves as the Chesil Bank itself, against the destroying sea.

REEDS ON THE FLEET

THE SWANNERY, ABBOTSBURY

From the saltmarshes round Britain's shores to the tops of the Scottish mountains, our wildlife is being destroyed to the point where the once common is now rare, much that was rare is now extinct, and certain habitats have disappeared from whole counties or regions.

Since 1949, 95 per cent of our hay meadows have been destroyed; 80 per cent of chalk and limestone grasslands have been converted to arable or 'improved'; 50-60 per cent of lowland heaths have been ploughed up or have become scrubbed over through lack of grazing; 30-50 per cent of ancient broad-leaved woods have been converted to conifers or grubbed up to make more farmland; 50 per cent of lowland wetlands have been drained; and probably 30 per cent of upland heaths and grassland have been afforested, drained or treated with fertilizers.

To these man-made losses must be added those inevitably produced by the forces of nature which are constantly eroding the landscape, most particularly round the coast. The cliffs on either side of Lyme Regis on the border of Devon and Dorset and on the south coast of the Isle of Wight are geologically unstable and constantly slip into the sea, taking grassland, scrub and woodland with them. The coastlines of the Holderness in east Yorkshire, of north Lincolnshire and east Suffolk are being cut into by currents which sweep southwards down the North Sea.

But however great the losses due to nature, she, unlike man, always compensates. The crumbling cliffs of the east coast have been deposited further south as the spit of Spurn Head, the sandy beaches of Gibraltar Point and the complex of shingle ridges round Orfordness – each now an area rich in wildlife, embracing nature reserves of national importance. On the south coast the chalk and limestone cliffs of Beer and Lyme have been carried by the action of the waves up the Channel to contribute to the Chesil Bank.

The lesson is clear. We too must learn to follow nature's habitats to compensate for the horrendous losses of the last thirty-five years. Ecologists now have sufficient understanding of the interrelationships of plants and animals to make it possible to build simple communities such as water's edge and old grassland wherever opportunities arise. Progress has already been made. Gravel pits at the edge of expanding towns such as Milton Keynes and Peterborough – artefacts of their construction – have been planned and planted to add enjoyment of wildlife to their leisure facilities. A few local authorities, such as Basildon in Essex, are sowing wild flower seeds on the banks of new roads to gladden the eye and encourage the butterflies. This practice could be adopted on new roads throughout the country; likewise, when boundary hedges are planted they could be composed of a mixture of shrubs to provide food and shelter for birds and insects.

By positive planning and management many thousands of acres of water, grassland and hedgerow could be transformed into wildlife habitats which, though never entirely replacing what we have destroyed, would ensure that the sounds, scents and sights of nature will continue to be a vivid part of living in Britain.

THE CHESIL BANK NEAR ABBOTSBURY

THE WILTSHIRE DOWNS

GEOFFREY GRIGSON

By accident and by choice I have lived for most of my life in landscape of two kinds, a shut landscape and an open one, the landscape of east Cornwall and the landscape of north Wiltshire, on the edge of downland and Salisbury Plain. The Cornish landscape belongs to childhood, the Wiltshire landscape to maturity, and different as they are, I have discovered in them a common affective element.

My Cornwall was much divided, deep valleyed country, through which roads were overgrown lanes still of a narrowness more suitable for pack-animals. These deep water-mint valleys or coombes – one of them began in our steep-sided garden – twisted to the sea, which can never be far away in Cornwall, and is suddenly encountered in openings between cliffs.

My Cornish landscape is a secret one, though villages and churches are close to each other; my Wiltshire landscape is an open one, the villages far apart.

Going back to Cornwall and its secretiveness, which I seldom do, I am rather horrified – if that isn't too big a word – to find in my old love for such an environment more of an inherited, historical character, less of a personal character than I like. From a reading lately of the first volume of Maurice Cranston's reconsideration of Jean-Jacques Rousseau, I realize how very much

THE DOWNS NEAR BARBURY CASTLE, WILTSHIRE

Rousseau's formulated preference in surrounding landscape has determined our own. Rousseau, that new European sensibility, with his sparkling eye, was all for mountain, crag, rock, waterfall, storm, for the involuted and convoluted. He wrote, when he was living below the Alps at Chambéry, in the Savoy, that 'Flat country, however beautiful it might be, has never seemed beautiful to me'. And here am I rejecting the Cornish miniature version of Rousseau's preference, if not plumping, exactly and totally, for the opposite.

My discovery of Wiltshire of the plain, half a century ago, led me to some degree of anti-romantic apostacy, of anti-Rousseauism. It began with a walk – a weekend escape out of London – from a station near Devizes, over sheep downland, to Avebury; from which I remember, not so much enigmatic standing stones, as a width of sky and slope and view, to an accompaniment, as it happened, of sheep-bells.

Lighten our darkness, lighten our secretiveness.

My apostacy was gradual, and has remained incomplete. I first came to live in Wiltshire, not long after, in a romantic or sub-Rousseauistic situation, under an escarpment, embossed with the velvet of tree clumps, a highway for moons full or crescent in the mode and the mood of Samuel Palmer whom I wrote about when he was still more or less unknown. But nowadays it is up to the downland that I go. I think to claim that this undramatic openness of landscape (which is rare for England) has 'influenced my writing' might be specious. Perhaps what can be claimed genuinely in that regard is becoming associated with a new landscape more or less in harmony with a discovered or recognized self. Or is it specious to say that in width each of us, as writers especially, may find a mental opening and growing up, a deprovincialization of interests, a rejection of a cosy, dangerous hiding away?

Anyhow, the affective element I valued and found in different ways, different degrees both in that secret Cornish milieu and the open Wiltshire milieu, was – and how old-fashioned a word it seems now – loneliness or solitude. In Cornwall car-parks have become too close, too ubiquitous for a genuineness of solitude such as I could find and feel once in a narrow water-mint slad visited by no one except myself, and a farmer in search of his heifers. In Wiltshire sunlight gleams off cars by the hundred parked at Avebury or Stonehenge, notices say 'Tank crossing', dogs from the town are being exercised, parents and children are playing with metal detectors, motor cycles rev and roar and slide along green tracks, red hang-gliders are floating into vales. But it remains country in which selective solitude is more possible.

In general, though, how is a necessary selective solitude to be maintained, without social affront? Improved agriculture eliminates poppies. Who is to tell farmers to do less well in the interests of 'spiritual' requirement?

A solution seems impossible, now that we have so increased our numbers, our means of transport, and our general destructiveness. I recommend one way of discovering what we have lost, and are still losing. Turn from plate to plate by William Daniell in the four volumes of *A Voyage round Great Britain* (1825) and compare a headland, say, or a harbour landscape which Daniell depicted for its charms in that era of Wellington and Waterloo and Wordsworth and Constable, with its present appearance smothered in houses precisely for love of a view which the smothering has destroyed.

Sitting and talking not so long ago with a Polperro fisherman (at least I suppose he still fished), and looking down on the quays, I discussed Polperro of my childhood as a place still of semi-solitude, compared with Polperro where we have to push through the alleys past gift shops. 'Well,' he said, 'you had it all your own way. Now they're having their share.' Unanswerable. No solution, no general solution.

Certainly Wiltshire – downland Wiltshire, which is the greater part of this ancient area – is going to retain a fair degree of emptiness and visible distance, in spite of the cars. Emptiness more or less is certainly going to survive in those great tracts which won't be controlled for ever by the War Department. I look forward to the day when the army camps in sight of Stonehenge will be pulled down, leaving downland Wiltshire a fair chance of entire renewal, if only because no other conglomerates of building and habitation are going to find cause for existence across what remains, on the whole, as for the last six thousand years, a vast sheep-walk.

Well protected antiquities add to the pleasures of this loneliness in time

STONE CIRCLE, AVEBURY

NETTLES AND THISTLEDOWN, FYFIELD DOWN

SWEET CHESTNUTS, SAVERNAKE FOREST

and in space. If you cut across the downland from prehistoric Avebury to medieval and modern Devizes you cut through Wansdyke – Woden's Dyke, the ditch and rampart of the high god of the Anglo-Saxons. Near this point on the dyke, on 11 June 1613, a Wiltshire clergyman, George Ferobe, made his shepherd parishioners perform a masque before Queen Anne, consort of James I, on her return from Bath to London. It included mention of 'the wide, wild houseless downs'. That is a good phrase. They are still wide, still wild more or less, and still more or less without houses. For the values of loneliness I like to think they will remain so – probably – for another 370 years; or another 6000 years.

The majority of the low hills which shape the landscape of south and east England are made of chalk, forming distinctive rounded downs and wolds. Until three hundred years ago their three million acres were mostly covered in short, herb-rich turf, the product of centuries of close grazing by millions of sheep. Today only 100,000 acres (3 per cent) remain, and much of that is threatened by human activity – or lack of it. Grazing sheep keep coarse grasses under control and allow the growth of small and attractive wild flowers. When grazing stops, even temporarily, tall vigorous grasses such as upright brome take over, eliminating low-growing, less competitive species. Longer neglect leads to invasion by woody shrubs, and eventually the grassland disappears beneath a dense thicket of hawthorn or dogwood.

Intensification of agriculture may be equally destructive. The use of selective herbicides, the application of artificial fertilizers and the sowing of commercial grasses in the wild turf all contribute to eliminating the majority of wild flowers. But, since the Second World War, it is the plough which has buried the sweet-scented sward – beneath a sea of barley. In Dorset 20,000 acres of downland in the 1930s was down to only 5,000 in the 1970s. Today, unless they have been acquired as nature reserves, sites survive only where the slopes are too steep to cultivate or they fall within military ranges. These combine in Wiltshire to make it the pre-eminent county for chalk grassland in the kingdom: 70 per cent of what remains of this habitat in England falls within its boundaries. Just under half of Wiltshire's 75,000 acres lie within Ministry of Defence land, while the rest occur on steep valley sides and scarp slopes.

Even in this exceptional county three-quarters of the remaining sites are small and isolated, with areas of less than 50 acres. What was once a continuous carpet has been broken up into a scatter of small mats. Such fragmentation leads to further impoverishment. Surrounded as they are by agricultural land these downland islands are exposed to damage, especially along the margins, from insecticides, herbicides, fertilizers and other modern farm chemicals. This accidental spray-drift leads to the loss of plant and animal species. Furthermore, because they are isolated from other areas of chalk grassland most 'lost' species cannot return by migration across the alien farmland habitat, except in areas where a network of green lanes and protective hedgerows remains. These not only provide highways for humans but act as connecting links along which plants and animals can travel. Their removal impoverishes the landscape and simultaneously adds still further to the problems of conserving one of our most rapidly dwindling wildlife assets.

THE MANGER, NEAR UFFINGTON

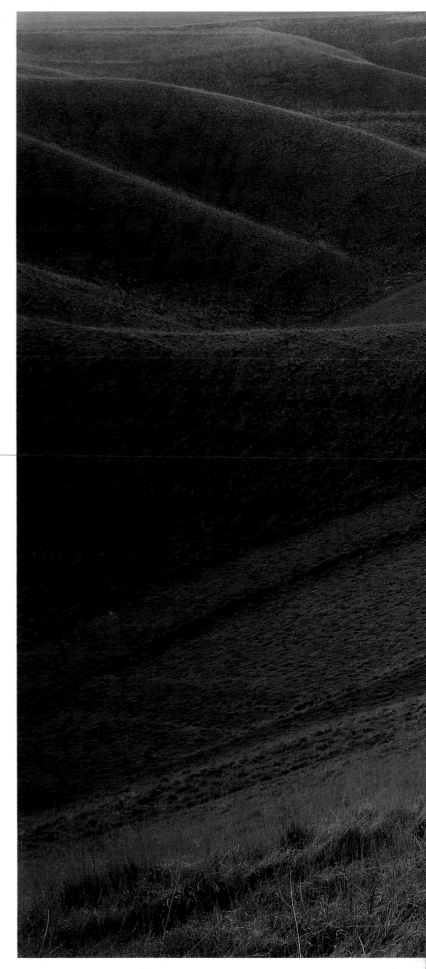

CHICHESTER HARBOUR

RICHARD WILLIAMSON

In August the hot sands of Chichester harbour are drenched twice daily by the tide, rising unnoticed as I wander with bare feet and trousers rolled to the knee. Cool water plunges around the ankles, bubbles of warm air breaking from the sand effervesce between the toes. Feet tired of man-made fibre socks, of rubber soles, of pavements and city streets, rejoice. The mind relaxes. The mind feels strong. It looks at the water's edge, mesmerized by the flattening and smoothing away of other people's footmarks, of the darkening and varnishing of pebbles. It looks along the ribbon of bubbles to where the sea begins. There is a great glassy slide of water out there, a curve going out of sight like the back of a leviathan. That is the power curve of the ocean, bulging and extending, feeling the land of France, of Africa, or the cold far lands of Russia. This is wilderness, which much of our land has lost. One feels it in mountains still. It is drawn from the mountains by the rivers to harbours, estuaries and coastal marshes which are the nerve-endings of a system that connects the mind to distance.

Now it is October. Last sails of the season drift like icebergs. Quietly the harbour empties, exposing tawny sand-bars and shoals of mud. It is not the mud of fighting or misery. It is the mud of life and of light, focused and rearranged light which has already scattered or bounced from clouds or water:

SALTMARSH AT EAST HEAD, CHICHESTER HARBOUR, SUSSEX

the alchemy is astounding. It is a prism, inverting, inventing, blending, bending in blue, or blue-grey, or bluey grey-green.

A few hours later, in darkness, the moon has risen over the muds. The movement of gold water in the channels, of gold curves and black shadows and the sudden glimpse of wildfowl teeming, is as thrilling as the first sight of an Eastern city. Many October nights I have sat on the sea wall till the early hours, watching the sea altering moment by moment as the moon traverses the wintry sky, altering finally to a white glare as the tide floods under the brightest moon of the year. This is *La Mer,* and *Peter Grimes.* Curlews call with their memory of summer on the moors, and this is the *Catalogue d'oiseaux.* All that is best in the world that I have seen and heard is released again. There are three thousand acres of the harbour, enough to make many tons of butter, thousands of gallons of milk, if we rid ourselves of this desire for music.

Do the many people who criss-cross this harbour in their boats hear the music? Do they realize how intricate is the detail that produces this panacea? Or is it to them only a playground? No matter. Their interests do not conflict with the natural world. The money they are prepared to spend on their luxury helps, unbeknown to them, to keep this place as a wilderness. Take away the tide by barrage and the shapes and colours are gone. Industrialize it, and agriculturalize it; allow the many billion animals in the living muds to die by pollution and that mud will become sullen, its gleam lost, as on a dead salmon.

Once I longed to travel in the remote polar regions of Russia, to see the masses of waterfowl, and know that I was on the roof of the world. Now, in winter, with a Russian wind hissing in the marrams, I can be there even so. The harbour is deserted by all those who think of it merely as a playground. The harbour is deserted. But the wildfowl are there in thousands, the wildfowl who keep themselves alive here on their winter holiday from the Arctic wastes. The tide is grey and white, bringing in a scum of grass and reeds. Brent geese rise from nearby fields and spread themselves across the sky in lines, one line above another, rising, falling; a block of black birds, dense as the final pages of a symphony score. The eye strains to follow them, the ear fancies it can hear the boom and grind of ice-floes in their calls. Another connection to distance, which is freedom. Everywhere, on these tidal places, I am reminded of the mass of life on our planet. Shore birds turn and wheel in shoals, like fish in some newly discovered South Sea paradise. Are there five thousand, or ten? Casually they turn and every white belly glances in the sun. Turn again and they are as a smoke plume from a great liner. Again, and they vanish. They weft and warp, unrehearsed but perfect, playing with shapes in the sky. Look at one bird through a powerful glass. A thousand feathers overlap, each different in shape, to waterproof, to glide, to propel, to slide through the air on terrible journeys to Iceland, or Greenland, or Spitsbergen, and back. They are perfect, and this is their place, on these lonely winter waters.

Look at the shoreline after the tide has gone and see the necklace many miles long of sea life formed, lived, and broken up, the ossuary of the oceans; of shells and seaweeds and crustaceans, and eggs of strange creatures as yet undreamed of by most of mankind, altered and renewed daily, to be reformed and used again.

And summer is still to come. The fretting waves of winter will go, and the changing shades of grey will take on colour. I will lie in the sandhills and let slip the grains million by million and feel relaxation in stroking the earth. There will be a buoyant air from the Azores, and azure lines with white froth in the sea and in the air. The air will draw with it the swallows, and the sea swallows, cuckoos and pipits, warblers and hobbies; all will land tiredly among the hills and rest, feed, and fly on into England. Plants will show flowers as small as stars: sea milkwort, stonecrop, sandwort, spurrey; the mind conjures up the names like a huntsman numbering his hounds.

Here I will lie in the sun, where I now crouch against the cold, and touch the hot sand and all its tiny plants and feel the charge of my mother earth. I know that as one of the creatures here, my body moving and being is as amazing as all the others. And as they need this place to live, so do I. I need this contact with the earth, with more than the earth, with the nerves that stretch out from the earth; that stretch through the seas and the skies, that stretch through all that is known of this earth, and that stretch into those

THE ESTUARY, CHICHESTER

SAND DUNES, EAST HEAD

regions that are still unknown. I think we all need this contact, however hard a deal we drive with the devil; perhaps not all the time, perhaps only once a month, or less, perhaps once a year, or perhaps even only once in a lifetime.

It may be that our choice of habitat is formed in childhood – my soul's seedtime was the marshes, and so it is to the marsh that I turn to refresh myself. Sometimes it is enough to see it from a car window, sometimes even just to know it is there. But to know that it had gone, that next summer, and the next winter, I would not be able to come down to this estuary, would not be able to walk over the sands with the wind flattening the skin into my cheeks, would no longer see and hear the wildfowl with their wild, harsh calls, would no longer be able to sit and stare into space – this would be to have that gleam of the mind, or soul, or whatever sacred area we call our own, crushed and replaced with a dreadful dull depression and a will not to live.

MARRAM GRASS IN THE SAND AT EAST HEAD

The saltmarshes and mudflats of Britain's estuaries and sheltered bays have long been subject to embankment and reclamation for agriculture. The Romans began the process when they separated the Fens from the Wash, and sea walls around our coast still bear witness to centuries of such enclosure.

The twentieth century has brought its own destructive forces to further diminish this wilderness. Since 1950 the pace of change has quickened. The Nature Conservancy Council has calculated that in thirty years up to 1980 14,000 acres of the 94,000 acres (15 per cent) which existed in 1950 has been reclaimed and in some areas, like the Wash, up to 40 per cent has become farmland. Saltmarshes near large ports have been prime targets for industrial development, and the growth of leisure and the desire to 'muck about in boats' has created a demand for new yacht basins and their associated marina villages. Industry and leisure each produce waste, and thousands more acres near these developments have disappeared under layers of refuse.

Agriculture, industry and leisure have combined in two estuaries to obliterate virtually all the saltmarshes and mudflats they once embraced. At Teesmouth, in the North East, the last 350 acres in an estuary which in 1800 contained 6000 acres is now subject to development, while in Southampton Water, only twenty miles west of Chichester Harbour, most of what little remains has been allocated to industry.

Industry, roads and tips are outward and visible signs of change; with them come less obvious but equally destructive agents in various forms of pollution. Nutrient-enriched domestic and industrial effluents have stimulated the growth of green algae which blanket the mud in summer: this has increased the food supply for geese and wigeon but reduced the area available for some mud-probing waders, thus altering the balance of the bird population. Waders may also be threatened by a build-up of heavy metals in the mud and all estuarine birds near oil terminals and harbours are in constant danger of oil spills.

The almost total loss of the saltmarshes in two of Britain's estuaries should be sufficient warning, but in 1980 29 of our 41 largest intertidal areas were subject to proposals for a different kind of development. One of these proposals presents a new threat which would eclipse in scale any others yet devised for Britain: the Severn Barrage would, if built, have a devastating effect on the saltmarshes upstream, quite apart from the inevitable industrial growth which would follow. And somewhere 'in the air', above either the Severn or the Thames estuary, hangs the shadow of a third London airport which, as planned for Maplin Sands, would engulf over 15,000 acres of estuary now used as wintering grounds by dark-bellied brent geese.

The future of these saltmarshes and mudflats is not the concern of the British alone. We are bound by international agreements to protect wetlands of worldwide ornithological importance. If we allow this erosion to continue we shall lose not only the geese and the waders but our reputation as a nation which cares about its wildlife.

SAND-BARS AT LOW TIDE, CHICHESTER HARBOUR

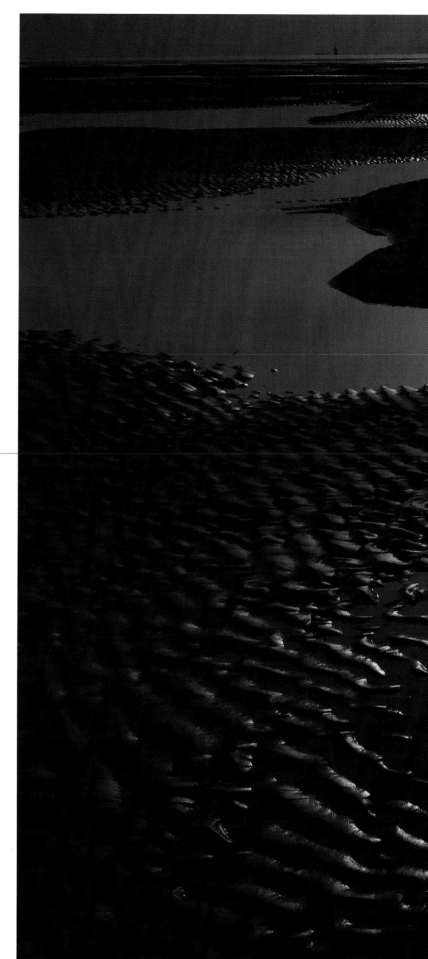

A SUFFOLK VALLEY WOOD

RONALD BLYTHE

Childhood is, among so much else, a matter of attainable destinations. That early getting about on one's own two feet is a thrilling business. Woods of all shapes and sizes were high up on my desirable destinations list. There were plenty to choose from, although none of them actually spectacular. According to books, woods were where the action was and my heart used to race and thump when I reached them. A few steps into a wood altered all this, switched my expectancy. Its silence, which was really the amalgamated sound of its murmurings and snappings, instantly transformed me from adventurer to contemplative. Except that to prop one's bike against a roadside tree and walk in and in and in needed quite a bit of physical daring as well as that state of mind which, at home, was referred to as 'his mooning'. Serve them right if, poignantly, there were banner headlines shouting, 'LOST BOY'S BICYCLE FOUND AGAINST OAK. WOOD CLAIMS ANOTHER VICTIM'.

When ones comes to think about it, the sole purpose of woods in children's literature is as places to get lost in. It was both a relief and a disappointment to the nine-year-old me to wander half a mile through a Suffolk wood and suddenly step out into a land of non-wood and familiar bearings. Also, it now occurs to me, our local woods were apt to get rather crowded at certain times of the year, bluebell time, blackberry time and just 'wooding' time, when

ELM BARK, ASSINGTON WOOD, SUFFOLK

people of all ages could be seen lugging home the spoils. These were always hauled off in quite immoderate quantities: bluebells in such arm-loads that they slipped steadily for miles, blackberries heaped into fishbags until they soaked through the straw, mutilated fungus (it is strange how so many people are compelled to break a fungus) and a good log which someone couldn't carry another yard. Woods were universal providers of nuts, fruit, fuel, flowers, holly, mistletoe, birds' eggs and so on, and were not then noticeably infested with gamekeepers. Lovers, of course. Woods made girls uneasy and boys brave. 'Going bluebelling' would usually raise a laugh. A gypsy or two might be encamped on the verges. 'My mother said, that I never should/Play with the gypsies in the wood.' Chance would have been a fine thing. They were so exclusive, so unreachable. Their dogs barked but they themselves never said a word.

The wood I liked best was six miles away and was variously referred to as Assington Wood, Assington Thicks, Agar Fen and Tiger Hill, the latter because the tooth of a tiger had been found there. It covered a deep little valley and had a lane running through the middle of it. There was never the least doubt when you reached it that you had come to somewhere very special. A swift, gravelly stream hurried through this ever-fascinating wood on its way to the Stour, and ran bridge-less across the road itself so that everybody had to splash through it. There were also nightingales, 'thick on the ground', as an old woman strangely said, although we knew what she meant.

Almost a lifetime later I find myself within sight of this beloved childhood wood from a house on the south bank of the Stour. Seen from such a distance of time and cornfields, it looks formidable. But when I walk to it, it gradually dissolves from being a dark massif into its old pleasant self. More than ever it constitutes an important destination. It is amazingly unchanged, and because visiting it is less like going back than just going on, I suddenly felt the need to take some kind of stock. It was warm mid-October and a good moment to make an inventory. No nightingales but a yaffle among the diseased elms whose crowns had snapped off, so that they looked like the shelled trees of the Western Front. No blackberries still fit to eat but plenty of sloes and cerise

WOODLAND MOSAIC, ASSINGTON WOOD

OAK AND BUCKLER FERN, ASSINGTON WOOD

spindleberries. Leaves everywhere were thinning but not yet down, and made their special fleshless autumn sounds, the poplars most of all. There were token remnants of summer flowers, red campion particularly. Nettles which only a month ago would have barred the way lay vertical to the earth but were raising soft, fresh branches from their tumbled old stems, and there was woody nightshade in abundance. Startling even amongst so much turning foliage were the intense crimson leaves of the wild cherry, a tree which John Evelyn called 'mazzards'. The wood was warm, even snug. 'One impulse from a vernal wood', wrote Wordsworth (had he in mind that profoundly wooded year at Alfoxden?) could teach one more than 'all the sages can', and the impulse which Assington generates, if that is the word, is, I now recognize, intellectual. Here is every grade of existence from soaring bird to mulch. This is a lightly managed wood which is wayward and a might rough. It is the kind of woodland which travellers to almost anywhere once had to blunder through, a thriving mile or two of an earlier England, a woodland like that painted by Gainsborough in the 1740s at Cornard, which is just up the road.

Assington Wood has always been and continues to be genuine woodlanders' territory. A few families, hidden from each other but whose voices sometimes carry through the trees, have lived in it for centuries. Its modest architecture manages to survive the general dampness and verdour and remains solid enough. The buildings consist of a little farmhouse with pointed windows, its tall cart-shed gaping trustingly on to the lane and crammed with retired implements, and two or three labourers' cottages. The wood in fact is a tye, or a minute centre of population far from the main village. It must have bred a distinctive people who lived well on rabbits, birds, fruit and pure water. Their warrening, draining, lopping pursuits still mark every foot of the area. It is due to their efforts that Assington offers its intriguing mixture of total wildness and ancient hand-marks. The small, flinty fields cultivated all round the wood have now been pulled into one or two vast fields, still very stony, and the bracken warned off for good. But the occasional sarsen lies by the field-edge, just as it did long ago. And the wood itself juts in and out of the corn in such a way that some of the fields are like three-sided rooms with huge green and brown walls. The adjoining pastures have remained as they were and cap each other in a series of succulent humps, like the cheerful meadows in a child's picture-book. John Nash, who painted all round here, referred to this landscape as the Suffolk–Essex Highlands. These woods never look better than they do in late October, when the penultimate moment of their summer density is scored across this border countryside of new wheat and drillings, sharp distances and vivid skies.

It is usual to be badly let down when one returns to the scenes of youthful excitement, but not so at Assington. These woods do not lure me even one single step towards mind-weakening nostalgia – which is what I expected when I returned to them. I think it is because they have so much going on in them at the moment that they divert one from the past. Even more than the fields – which in any case now seen to have acquired a computerized motion – old, personal-to-one's-self woodlands like Assington–Agar Fen–Tiger Hill possess that powerful cyclic movement which gives a kind of reflective zest to the present. 'Enter these enchanted woods, you who dare,' wrote Meredith in his poem 'The Woods of Westermain', and that is it: the daring to enter what is in effect the jurisdiction of the forest. This modest wood of, perhaps, some fifty acres has always suggested to me a sampling of the forest proper in many of its varieties. It *was* the forest proper when I was a boy. Now it is a sequence of glades, sluices, stands of ash, oak and beech, gardens, flowery banks, scrub, conifers, rabbit runs, tracks – anything a visiting woodlander can ask for.

With the exception of relatively small areas of pine woods in the Highlands of Scotland and yew woods on limestone and chalk in the south and west of Britain, the natural vegetation cover of these islands below the tree line is broad-leaved deciduous woodland. The majority had already been cleared for agriculture by Domesday, and woods only remained where they were of value to the community or too difficult or remote to clear. Almost every parish retained a wood through the Middle Ages, managing it as a source of timber for buildings and for implements, for firewood, fruits and game – a self-sustaining harvest of a wild crop. Larger areas like the New Forest or Rockingham Forest were retained, often by royalty, for fox and deer hunting.

The importance of woodland for the landscape was not fully appreciated until the eighteenth century, whereas a consciousness of its value for wildlife did not emerge until the beginning of this century, by which time half the Domesday woodlands had already been lost to arable and pasture. But no sooner had pioneer conservationists begun to appreciate the variety and wealth of our ancient woodlands than a new threat developed with the establishment of the Forestry Commission in 1919. This body not only planted forests of alien trees in our uplands but also converted lowland woods into plantations of needle-producing, wildlife-blanketing larch, pine and spruce. Beauty, amenity and nature conservation alike were swept aside as maximum timber production became the primary goal. In addition to such direct activities the Commission was able, through a widespread system of grants, to persuade many private landowners to follow suit, a process helped by a variety of tax concessions made available by the Government.

Thus, despite a growing awareness of the importance of our ancient woodlands for their scientific, educational and historical features, their rate of destruction has accelerated. Since 1946, 30-50 per cent of them have been cleared or converted into conifer plantations. If this process continues, we shall over a brief period in the history of our islands have witnessed the conscious vandalism of a part of our national heritage as savage and irresponsible as an intruder cutting all the Turners in the Tate to ribbons or smashing all the medieval glass in York Minster. For once destroyed, these ancient woodlands cannot be re-created: their rich associations of plants and animals, their rare and sensitive species, the local history locked in their banks and ditches, and their thousand-year-old coppiced hazels will have gone for ever. Future generations will rightly point their finger with anger and amazement at an age in which millions had their eyes opened by *Life on Earth* on television while allowing its wonders to be destroyed in the real world beyond their curtained windows.

HONEY FUNGUS, ASSINGTON WOOD

THE FENS

EDWARD STOREY

Today would have been a good day to introduce a stranger to the Fen country: the pale mauve sky of daybreak quickly brightening to a crystalline blue and the landscape coated in that pure light which is a feature of this corner of England.

Light . . . space . . . far distances . . . sky . . . how can one describe this unique and predominately man-made landscape? Some people would, I know, use words such as 'dull', 'flat' and 'colourless'. Not me, especially on such a late spring morning as this. Having spent my life in this kingdom of mists, harvest fields and open country, I know there can be days when the fields look uninvitingly soggy, when the grey clouds sag more like wet sacks and the horizon disappears into a blurred bleakness which can depress. But today the light magnifies and extends all boundaries. This morning the land is shining as if every blade of grass or leaf of new crop is lit from within. Whitewashed farm-buildings twelve miles away stand out with a brilliant clarity as if carved out of snow. Snow would not survive long today, for the air is warm and the dazzle on the land comes from a sun unimpeded by mist or industrial smoke.

You cannot ignore the sun in the Fens. It rises over the eastern ridge of the world in the early morning and continues its regal journey across the great continent of sky, holding court for a moment at the noon's zenith, before its

BURNT FEN, CAMBRIDGESHIRE

WOODWALTON FEN

slow procession to the westerly horizon. There are not many places in Britain where you can witness such a complete arc of the sun's path. It is omnipresent and we are its subjects.

So, yes, we have light, space, distance and sky perhaps unequalled in this country. But there is more. After writing thousands of words on these virtues I still find it difficult to describe adequately the intangible qualities which give my native landscape its special character and appeal. Where then do I begin to justify my claims for it again, or explain the excitement and love I feel for a countryside whose beauties may not be apparent to the casual eye? It is, I admit, an elusive, shy, almost hidden country which is not easy to discover, but it is one worth getting to know a little better.

Do I proceed with these rhapsodic impressions or rely on facts? There must be a little of both. Statistics and historical events in themselves can do no more than present a loom on which to weave a personal interpretation of a country's charm. I have said elsewhere that no part of England can be isolated into a weekend or be judged by a season, least of all the Fen country. A wet sugar-beet season can turn paradise into purgatory. The north-east winds of winter can be pitiless and the frosts will gnaw hungrily into the bones of anyone exposed to those arctic spaces. But in April and May when the oil-seed rape fields are a startling yellow, when the air grows inebriant with the smell of meadowsweet and the acres of barley flow with a silken rustle, there is nowhere to give one a greater sense of pride in man's achievement on the land.

I emphasize man's role in the making of this landscape because it was not always so. There was a time when the Fens rightly earned their name and reputation. Daniel Defoe was not being unkind or inaccurate when he described them as 'the sink for thirteen counties'. Water flowing down from the uplands could not be contained within the winding rivers of the Great Ouse, Nene and Welland. Their banks burst and thousands of acres were constantly under flood. The natural basin formed by the geological eccentricities of time meant that the water, having arrived, could not then flow uphill to the outfalls in the Wash. The problem was often aggravated by

FODDER FEN

the sea walls breaking at high tide so that salt water made its own claims upon the enormous wilderness of marsh and fen. It has taken the ingenuity and vision of man to transform this scene of desolation into the fertile region we can praise today.

This is not the place in which to enlarge on Fen drainage, that fascinating drama of man's struggle with the elements. It is, after all, only part of the history which has gone into the making of the modern Fen country we know today. The Romans, Anglo-Saxons, Scandinavians, Normans and Dutch have also left their influences. Canute, Hereward the Wake, Cornelius Vermuyden and Oliver Cromwell are only some of the characters in the events which have contributed to our story.

As I drove the other day through a world of emerald green fields and saw the solitary figures of men scattered across the land hoeing their sugar-beet crops or harrowing, I knew that I must devote the space on these pages to an impression of what this area has meant to me – why I have spent my writing years exploring the meaning of 'belonging to a place', why I have been content to draw on its ancient springs for most of that writing. It is a land I have known since I was born in the Isle of Ely more than fifty years ago, a land in which I grew up surrounded, not only by the vast Cambridgeshire Fens, but also by the people who worked on the land. In those far off days I took that world of limitless space and extravagant skies for granted. I did not question why the land was so flat, the soil so black, the countryside so sparse of trees, the rivers so important. I imagined that the rest of the world was the same. I knew nothing of mountains, lakes, valleys or woodlands. My world was as flat and green as a billiard table. It belonged in essence to the wind and skylarks, herons and reed-mace. It was a world of newly ploughed furrows and wheatfields, of long, grass-bordered roads embroidered with dandelions, toad-flax, poppies, vetch and wild iris. Not for twenty years did I realize that the Fens were different, and it was even longer before I appreciated the importance of the relationship which is slowly established between a man and his landscape.

But is the 'spirit of place', I began to wonder, something we create for our

REEDS AND WILLOW, WOODWALTON FEN

own needs, projecting our feelings into the landscape, making *it* accept us rather than *we* accept it? Or does the landscape itself have a spirit which we learn to recognize, absorb, interpret and draw from until, in the end, we are unmistakaby shaped or conditioned by the very nature of the soil from which we come?

I found the answer in Laurens van der Post's book *Jung and the Story of Our Time,* in which he recalls how the great thinker told him repeatedly that 'the nature of the earth itself has a profound influence on the character of the people born and raised on it . . . ' Jung could not offer any scientific proof that this was so but, from his lifetime's study of people, he maintained that a character became an expression of the soil.

Many of the characters I have known and written about were to confirm this view for me, and I began to feel that I was part of a long (and largely unwritten) tradition. The people I knew were undoubtedly 'expressions of the soil', especially those who had lived and worked in the Fens for most of their lives. They had that far-distant look in their eyes, that quiet but belligerent response to life that has known all the vicissitudes of nature – the cruel winters and the beneficent summers, the winds, floods, seasons and harvests which they have learned how to conquer and control, creating this landscape which we can now enjoy. Whether they work with animals or machines, they are the living evidence of Jung's belief. They are an integral part of the land just as the land is part of them. Their behaviour and their attitudes are conditioned by it and, one hopes, always will be.

Since I began writing about the Fens much has, inevitably, changed – sometimes for the better, sometimes not. Not only is the rich peatland (formed over thousands of years from an age when the Fens were as wooded as anywhere in England) shrinking to a disturbing level, but the demands of society today are also diminishing that land. Fields which were a feature of the landscape just ten years ago have now surrendered to the bulldozers and developers. Quiet lanes have become busy roads and minor roads have become dual carriage-ways. Farm machinery now costs four or five times what it did and the value of land has reached prices which, for our grandparents, would have bought half the country. East Anglia has become a fashionable place in which to live, and old-established communities are losing something of their traditional identity. But I can still reflect on the virtues of this land and find my feelings for it unchanged, my loyalties unaltered by time, my roots unsevered. Where else, I ask again, could I find this clarity of light and expanse of space to thrill the spirit as well as the eye? Where else could I feel so at home with the unending rituals of man and the soil, or be so at ease with an awareness of the past as well as the present?

Whether I travel between those 'once-upon-a-time' islands on which the great Fenland abbeys were built, or sit by rivers that have been tamed and straightened by modern engineers, I am conscious of being part of a daily pattern which has made sense not only of a place but of life itself. Would that stranger I spoke of at the beginning understand me a little better now or have a deeper appreciation of what this country means to me? I hope so.

> Today I met a man who shares
> My fascination with these fields.
> He said 'It is not what you see,
> It's what you know. Each furrow
> Is a lifeline on the hand. Each reed
> A symbol of our ancestry.' I stand
> And in the silence hear again
> Familiar voices rising from the ground.

I need no more than that assurance, no more than a day like this to remind me of who I am. Light . . . space . . . far distances . . . sky . . . and voices rising from the ground.

Every year, as a result of government-subsidized agricultural drainage and improvement schemes, up to 150,000 acres of wetlands in Britain are destroyed. Marshes and water meadows have disappeared at such a rate that in many lowland English counties only a handful now remain, and only those which are nature reserves are safe. Ironically the largest and most important of these runs through the heart of the Fens, from Earith to Denver, and is an artefact of their drainage by man.

The Ouse Washes is an area of 6000 acres of square fields and ditches lying between the straight cuts of the Old and New Bedford Rivers which are part of a scheme begun by Cornelius Vermuyden in the seventeenth century: over two-fifths is now owned and managed by the Wildfowl Trust, the Royal Society for the Protection of Birds and the Cambridgeshire Naturalists' Trust. The area acts as a temporary reservoir for flood water when the river Ouse is carrying more than can pass out to sea. This shallow 'lake' with its varying depths of water attracts up to 60,000 wildfowl in winter, teal, wigeon, pintail, mallard, shoveler and pochard being the most numerous. But of all the visitor the most important are the swans – not the resident black-billed mute swans but Bewick's and whoopers which breed in Scandinavia and north Russia and pass the winter in north-west Europe. The 2300 or so Bewick's which come to the Ouse Washes represent about 20 per cent of the world population of this handsome yellow-billed species.

The assembly of so many birds has for long attracted wildfowlers. In the past the majority were responsible members of Wildfowl Clubs who shot relatively small numbers of unprotected species, retrieved them with trained dogs, and learned more about ducks and swans during their long, cold vigils than most professed naturalists.

In the last ten years, however, the standard of shooting has fallen as the number of guns has increased. Many birds are shot at beyond killing range, and are thus 'pricked' which enables them to fly beyond the recovery range of the shooter, who rarely has a dog, so the birds die slowly and painfully. Totally protected species such as the Bewick's swan are also shot at: X-rays of captured birds show that 34 per cent of them carry lead pellets.

Another consequence of the growth of wildfowling has been the build-up of spent lead shot. The pellets move very slowly down through the soil and are thus likely to be picked up by wildfowl, a considerable number of which die each year from lead poisoning.

The problems are not unique to the Ouse Washes: they stem from a system which allows anyone with a gun to buy a day-ticket to shoot at wildfowl on private land. These 'cowboys', through ignorance or indifference, often fire at anything with feathers – even lapwings and skylarks are frequently killed. The only remedy is to institute a shooting test which must be passed by all those wishing to shoot wildfowl: it would include bird recognition and the law. In addition, shooting without dogs should not be allowed and steel shot should be obligatory in areas of heavy shooting to reduce the risks of lead poisoning.

THE WASH AND HUNDRED FOOT DRAIN

THE
BLACK
MOUNTAINS

JAN MORRIS

Some mountain ranges seem to have burst out of the earth's surface in exuberant explosion, taking the snow for their summits with them. Not Mynydd Du, the Black Mountains of south-eastern Wales, which lie in a brooding clump beside the English border, where Gwent, Powys and Herefordshire meet. They appear to have heaved themselves from the subterrain with infinite grave toil, and so they stand there with a sullen sort of beauty, geologically spent.

They are instantly recognizable. Whether you approach them out of England or out of deeper Wales, their long hunched silhouette stands like a rampart before you, apparently impenetrable – and if you should happen to approach them out of space, satellite photographs demonstrate, they show as a hefty blodge of brown like no other in sight. They are the most cohesive of the mountain massifs of Wales: ten miles long at their longest point, two and a half thousand feet at their loftiest cairn, never more than eight miles across, roughly oblong in shape and intersected only by three narrow valleys, two of them dead ends, in which perhaps five hundred people live. There are four churches hidden among them, four chapels, three pubs: there are several hundred ponies and what appear to be a couple of million sheep.

They are said to be called the Black Mountains because a combination of

WAUN FACH FROM DARREN LWYD, POWYS

THE BLACK MOUNTAINS FROM MYNYDD EPPYNT, POWYS

situation, light and foliage really does give them a sable look, shadowed with dark patches even in the sunshine: but they are metaphysically sombre too, full of wistful nuance. They are rather sad mountains: wonderfully beautiful, lyrical in some moods, sheep-speckled and wind-whistled, but sad.

There is something hallucinatory to their presence. Bracken covers most of the range, conifers lap the lower slopes, and those long twisting valleys, each with its fast-flowing stream, are sunk deep in the moorland. The air is utterly pure, except for mist, the light is pellucid, except when it drizzles, but something about the ordering of the whole, some particular refraction of atmosphere perhaps, makes scale and substance all illusory.

Take Mr Jones's farm – there, just to the left of the coppice, a small grey sprawl of stone, a barn with an iron roof, a tumble of tractors and half-dismantled cars, and Mr Jones himself, with his dogs, gathering the sheep in the field above (staccato shouts on the wind across the valley, chirp of whistle, scud of white woolly shapes across the meadow to the gate). He is not very far away, only half a mile or so, but he and his animals seem infinitely remote or reduced, all in crystal miniature. It is like looking through the wrong end of a telescope: some prism of the place puts not just Mr Jones, but all man's little works, permanently at a distance.

I sometimes think the church of the martyred St Isio, in the central valley of the three, is an illusion of an extremer kind, for if at one moment I can see it clear as daylight from my garden, at the next it seems to have vanished altogether. Is it really there at all? Often it seems no more than a dapple in the woods: and even when I have walked there, to make a wish at its holy well perhaps, or wonder once more at the red ochre skeleton upon the wall (painted so the local lore maintains in human blood) – once I have shut the churchyard gate behind me again, the trees close in once more and the light shifts, it is as though I have just imagined church, well, skeleton, martyred St Isio and all.

The web of time is looser here than in most places, too, and images tend to overlap. In a year or two cottages rebuilt as weekend retreats by Reading

GRWYNE FAWR, MYNYDD DU FOREST, POWYS

SPHAGNUM BOG, PENTWYNGLAS, POWYS

sociology lecturers, with Habitat bunks and Japanese paper lanterns, tend to look as utterly indigenous as the most shambled of the valley farms: and when the trekkers are out, and you see the long line of their ponies trailing across the flank of a hill, or tethered in the yard of the Rising Sun, they might just as well be the beasts of pack-horse men or medieval cavalry.

Even the fabric of the hills can be deceptive. Those gloomy stains on the moorland may resolve themselves, as you get nearer, into marvellous purple expanses of heather and bilberry: sometimes even the spare exhaustion of the Black Mountains turns out to have life and vigour after all, young horses are playing about up there on the ridges, grouse start in panic as you pass, and high above Disgwylfa, the Watching Place, skylarks sing in ecstasy.

Almost like tunnels the valleys thread their way into these hills, and they seem to invite secrets. For a few years in the 1920s a little steam train ran up and down the valley of the Grwyne Fawr, taking workers and materials to the reservoir at the top, but now no public transport reaches the Black Mountains. With their wild but compact intensity of form, so aloof to the pastoral country outside, they are like a refuge: you feel they could be locked off, with great steel gates at each valley mouth, for the containment of reclusives.

It was here they say that Dewi Sant, Saint David, set up his first hermitage beside the Honddu River, living on the wild leeks that were to become the symbol of his nation. Here the Augustinians came, in their search for the ideal solitude, to build the magnificent priory of Llanthony whose grey walls still stand there jagged and frondy – there is an inn in the old Abbot's house, and you may take your Real Ale, with a hamburger and chips, into the roofless ruin. Here too came, in the 1880s, the visionary Father Ignatius, to pursue convictions no less vivid, to see in fact the Virgin herself in a holly bush at Capel-y-Ffin, to establish his own community and to lie now, still visited by pilgrims, in his grave in the nave of its ruined chapel.

There is an air of sweet retreat to the little square church of Capel-y-Ffin, near the top of the Honddu valley, which Francis Kilvert the diarist likened to

MAT-GRASS ON PEN TRUMAU, POWYS

HAY BLUFF, OFFA'S DYKE, POWYS

AFON HONDDU, GWENT

an owl. There is a suggestion of raffish collusion to the derelict house of the Hermitage, at the top of the Grwyne Fach, in which we are told long ago a local swell maintained his mistresses. There is a disturbingly enigmatic power to the church of St Martin at Cwmyoy, which has been knocked all skew-whiff by subsidence or landslide, and stands there on its hillside altogether out of true, nothing perpendicular, nothing right-angled, nothing self-explanatory.

And about the scattered inhabitants of the hills, in the two hamlets of the Honddu, in the isolated farms and villages elsewhere, there is an unmistakable sense of withdrawal. Some of course are not true inhabitants at all, only weekend recreationists from England, but others have been here since the beginning of time, and seem enfolded in their mountains. Dark and hidden things still happen among them – incest, suicide, mental breakdowns, irreconcilable feuds over wills or boundaries – and the faces of the farmers are often set in a resentful mould, as though they suspect you of leaving a gate open: a gate not simply of their yard or sheep-pen, but of their sensibilities.

Prehistoric earthworks, east and west, guard the entrances to the Black Mountains, for if these hills have something of the quality of a haven, or a ghetto perhaps, they are also a natural fortress. They stand in country which was disputed for centuries by Welsh and English, and even now they are a kind of no-man's-land between cultures. When the Normans seized the rich Gwent lowlands in the twelfth century, the Welsh were mostly banished to higher, less productive, less accessible country: and nowhere was more proper for natives than the brackeny massif of the Mynydd Du, its valleys choked then with impenetrable forests of beech and oak.

Standing on several kinds of frontier – between countries, between counties, between languages, between dioceses, between languages – the Black Mountains have always been just the place for outlaws and recusants, and even now you might say that the central point of the whole range, the pivot around which its character and meaning revolves, is the old standing stone called Carreg Dial, the Stone of Revenge, which supposedly commemorates the one historic tragedy of these hills. Here in the year 1135 the Norman Earl of Clare, travelling to Talgarth from Y Fenni, Abergavenny, was ambushed by a commando of Welsh guerrillas, led by Morgan ap Owen of Caerleon. The Norman and his retainers were killed, every one, down to the very minstrel, in the dark woodlands which still stand thick above the Grwyne Fawr, and those susceptible to such things still feel a chill *frisson* when they pass that way, and fancy hatreds there.

Lovely though it looks to weekend visitors, in the hush of its remoteness, this has seldom been an innocent kind of country. According to Walter Savage Landor, who had property here in the 1800s, its people were then said to be the most lawless in Britain, and vagabond habits linger. Geese tend to be stolen shortly before Christmas; sheep are rustled; black-leather troops of motor cyclists sweep shatteringly through woodlands on bank holidays; rumours flit about, of fugitives hiding in upland barns, of criminals storing explosives, or distilling drugs, or making blue movies, in their dainty weekend cottages. The mountains welcome as their own the humped forms of the soldiers, their faces blackened, their guns slung, so often to be seen disappearing up the stony tracks, like Morgan ap Owen and his toughs before them, to rehearse their brutal craft.

Visitors from England, tramping the ridge-tracks of the Black Mountains, find the strange stillness of the place a consolation. Visitors out of Welsh Wales are more likely to find in it a haunting suggestion of abandonment. For though these mountains are in Wales, and offer landscapes as absolutely Welsh as you could find, long ago the living Welshness left them, and retreated further west, over beyond Brecon and Builth, into the hinterland. Hardly a soul speaks the Welsh language now: even Welsh radio and television, rebuffed by the high escarpment, does not reach these valleys.

But to a Welsh imagination there are echoes everywhere of the old lost culture, its style and its vocabulary. Up on the mountain I often imagine I hear the Welsh songs and banter of the cattle-drovers who used to pass this way out of the interior, stopping at inns that are now no more than piles of rubble, pounding their beasts in enclosures that are only unexpected patches of green among the bracken. It is easy to suppose those grey farms down there still with a harp in the parlour, and a poet at his books, and all too easy to think for a moment, when a distant voice sounds across the valley, that it is a cry in the old language — so all-but-Welsh does the dialect still sound, so close in intonation, if not in actual words, to that magnificent original!

Immediately to the south of the Black Mountains there stands a solitary outlier, Pen-y-Fal, the Sugar Loaf. This splendid peak is the very antithesis of the mountains themselves. It really does seem to have sprouted from the earth in an instant flowering of sandstone confidence, and it stands there grandly conical and commanding, looking southward, eastward, outward, anywhere but northward into the melancholy massif. On a breezy day of sunshine it is a fine thing to climb its summit and look down upon the rich vales of Gwent and Glamorgan, away to the shining strip of the Bristol Channel and easy green Somerset beyond.

For myself, though, I never face that way for long. Something always makes me turn, back towards the old bare hulk of Mynydd Du. Some nagging magnetism of those mountains compels me: as though there is unfinished, unspecified business awaiting me there, out of my own and my people's past.

Until the Second World War the gorse and heather covered hills of western Britain were a vivid contrast to the measured arable and grassland fields of the lowlands. Many of the plants and animals which had once been common everywhere, but were lost through drainage and cultivation in the lowlands, still survived in boggy valleys and unimproved moorlands, and there was a part of our islands where one could climb out of a human-infested, agrico-industrial landscape into a flowery wilderness disturbed only by the croak of ravens and the cry of curlew. In the last forty years that wilderness had been consistently eroded – for nothing.

During the war the need for this country to be self-sufficient in food was obvious. When the war ended, despite increasing opportunities to shop elsewhere, the theory persisted that we must maximize production, even from our marginal hill-lands where farming could never be profitable unless supported by huge subsidies.

So, over the years, successive governments have poured taxpayers' money into the hills to pay farmers to increase yields. Grants of 70 per cent have been available for field drainage and of 50 per cent to convert moorland rich in wildflowers to monotonous green pastures. To these have been added headage payments: for every cow kept the rate is currently £35, for every sheep £5.50. In all, 75 per cent of the income of hill farmers has come from grants to produce food which could have been bought more cheaply elsewhere, in the process destroying a wildlife heritage which can never be replaced.

The absurdity of this policy has become even more apparent since Britain joined the EEC and we found ourselves in a community producing surpluses. Even the relatively small amounts our hill-lands do create (about one-twelfth of the total output from 25 per cent of the land) contribute to butter-mountains and milk-lakes which, under Common Market rules, have to be bought at a guaranteed price, stored in expensive warehouses, and later sold at give-away prices.

This farce cannot be allowed to continue. Government must surely recognize that subsidies limited to the narrow objective of producing food we do not want must end, and that ways must be found to preserve the wilderness so that those who visit it may enjoy its peace and inspiration. Subsidies should be used instead to encourage farmers to play a part in protecting the beauty of the land they live on and conserving its wildlife. Funding must be channelled into rebuilding stone walls, improving footpaths, managing heather moors by traditional burning, maintaining unpol-luted ponds and streams, and planting copses for firewood and nesting birds. By these means the same amount of money which is now spent on destroying the uplands could be used to retain the wilderness for our enjoyment and to give wildlife another chance, while at the same time providing the farmer with a satisfying life and a decent livelihood.

THE VALE OF EWYAS, GWENT

A THICKET IN LLEYN

R.S. THOMAS

Leave it for me: a place in Lleyn, where I may repair to mend my feelings. Woods are scarce in Pen Llŷn, trees even. And this is only a thicket, but dear: 'Infinite riches in a little room.' It is, where I hide, where only the light finds me, filtering through the leaves in summer, and in winter the flash from a blade brandished by the sea nearby.

I watch the farm girl go by, unaware of me, and murmur to myself:

> *Blodau'r flwyddyn yw fy anwylyd,*
> *Ebrill, Mai, Mehefin hefyd,*
> *Llewyrch haul yn tywynnu ar gysgod*
> *A gwenithen y genethod.*

> (My love is all the months of the year,
> April, May, June too;
> the sun's light in a dark place,
> the wheat-germ among the girls.)

I approach it warily. It is nervous. Pfft! A sparrow-hawk is plucked from a branch, like an arrow from a bow. A magpie scolds, out of sight. The place sighs and is still. I wait, and tune my breath to its own. Is it autumn? A dead

MALE-FERN AND GOLDEN SAXIFRAGE, NEAR TAN-Y-GRAIG

leaf stirs and shows its red breast. Is it spring? There is a trickle of song from the bare twigs, where the first willow-warbler is newly arrived among the catkins, its throat also a catkin. In the small pool about the roots of the trees there is a movement, as frogs surface to regard me without change of expression on their primeval faces. So little by little the life of the thicket is resumed and I am forgotten. The dragon-fly quivers its wings in the light's rainbow, before bulleting off into the shade. A bird snaps its bill on an ephemeral insect. A luckier beetle runs unmolested up a tree's bark.

This is a thoroughfare for migrants, warblers in spring, thrushes in autumn. Once on a day in October, after the gales had stripped it, it was alive with goldcrests. The air purred with their small wings. To look up was to see the twigs re-leafed with their bodies. Everywhere their needle-sharp cries stitched at the silence. Was I invisible? Their seed-bright eyes regarded me from three feet off. Had I put forth an arm, they might have perched on it. I became a tree, part of that bare spinney where silently the light was splintered, and for a timeless moment the birds thronged me, filigreeing me with shadow, moving to an immemorial rhythm on their way south.

Then suddenly they were gone, leaving other realities to return: the rustle of the making tide, the tick of the moisture, the blinking of the pool's eye as the air flicked it; and lastly myself. Where had I been? Who was I? What did it all mean? While it was happening, I was not. Now that the birds had gone, here I was once again. Such things, no doubt, had occurred before and other humans had been present, had been a part of them for their own timeless moment, before returning to themselves, involuntary prodigals. Was this Coleridge's experience? To him, you remember, it was the imagination which was primary: 'a repetition in the finite mind of the infinite I AM.' Is that what had happened to me? Had that infinite I announced itself in a thicket in Lleyn, in the serenity of the autumnal sunlight, in the small birds that had taken possession of it, and in the reflection of this in a human being? And had the I in me joined seemingly unconsciously in that announcement; and is that what eternity is? And was the mind that returned to itself but finite mind?

There was something missing from all this. It was too like talk of the

SALLOW IN FLOWER NEAR NANHORON

AFON DWYFACH

MALE-FERN AND HART'S-TONGUE, NEAR NANHORON

PRIMROSES, GLYN-DWYFACH

minute drop returning to the boundless ocean. Such an interpretation smacked too much of the endlessly repeated life-cycle. 'That out of life's own self-delight had sprung the abounding, glittering jet', sang Yeats, memorably but how truthfully? Life is not I; is certainly not God. There is a conventional magnifying of life at the expense of the I. But what is that? Life feeds on life, and has an unconscious, inscrutable, repetitive quality. What talons and beaks were not in waiting for the goldcrests on their way south, to be themselves devoured later by the huge maw of the sea over which other goldcrests would return north on the spring passage?

No, while the experience lasted, I was absent or in abeyance. It was when I returned to myself that I realized that I was other, more than the experience, able to stand back and comprehend it by means of the imagination, and so by this act of creation to recognize myself not as lived by, but as part of the infinite I AM.

Lleyn is a peninsula, battered by wind and sea. There are a few small woods and thickets. Some of them even have names, Welsh names. I am not telling you where this one is, lest too many go there to deflower it. But leave it and others like it for the individual to have such experiences in. Maybe it is only a minute strand of the great web of being, but once broken it cannot be repaired. So with all the means available today do not uproot it or level it in an act of misplaced tidiness or improved farming. I see it as ribs of a body; body as the incarnation of spirit, and spirit returns to eternity and significance when it declares: I am, holding all things in balance; spiralling outward upon itself into infinite space and inward towards the smallest of atoms, awake or dormant in a thicket in Lleyn.

Hazel thickets and copses in the west of Britain often mark the site of ancient oakwoods long since felled, but within their shade they still shelter the relics of native woodland plant and animal communities which have survived on that very spot for several millenniums.

Hazel in a hedge is almost always an indication of its ancient origin, derived perhaps from adjacent woodland, now replaced by arable or pasture, but still accompanied by other woodland shrubs like holly, spindle and field maple and harbouring at their base woodland flowers such as bluebell, dog's mercury or wood anemone.

A landscape of knots of copse and strings of hedges provides a network of pathways along which woodland plants may spread and woodland animals can run and shelter. The widespread felling of copses and uprooting of hedges has not only disastrously damaged the landscape of Britain but has destroyed most of the wildlife which once enriched the sights and sounds of the countryside, leaving only small islands in a sea of arable or featureless grassland.

This process has been slower in the west of England, where copses and hedges are still valued by the livestock farmer as shelter for his sheep and cattle, and well-maintained hedges act as living stock-proof fences. In the east, however, where arable farms prevail and these features no longer have any farming function, thousands of acres of copses and tens of thousand miles of hedges have been grubbed up. Nevertheless in some areas a landscape of copses and hedges does remain, almost entirely due to the shooting or foxhunting interests of the owner or tenant. Copses provide cover and shelter for foxes, while a well-kept hedge makes an excellent jump. There is little doubt that if the anti-foxhunting lobby were successful many more copses and hedges would disappear and the interests of wildlife conservation would be further damaged.

Hedges are important for game preservation, especially where they have been laid to form a base of almost prostrate live branches through which new growth springs up. This produces a thick bottom which is an excellent nesting place for pheasants and partridges, while the plants and insects they harbour are a prolific source of food for adults and their chicks. Hedges also provide shelter for marksmen, hiding the guns from the birds and causing low-flying partridges in particular to rise into a position where they can be shot.

Although many people may be offended by this slaughter in our countryside, it must be remembered that most of the birds killed have been raised artificially and that the benefits to wildlife can be substantial, especially if the hedges are sympathetically managed. Ideally the hedges should be laid periodically and kept trimmed to heights of between four and seven feet, with work concentrated into late winter after all the berries have been eaten by the birds but before the nesting season begins.

If we want to retain in Britain a traditional landscape of copses and hedges in arable areas it may be necessary to find ways of paying farmers to maintain these features. A redistribution of grants to those farmers who recognize their importance to the landscape and wildlife is long overdue.

HAZEL AND RAMSONS, NEAR BODFUAN

THE LAKES

MELVYN BRAGG

'The prospect changes', wrote Thomas Gray, 'every ten paces.' He was writing, in the eighteenth century, of a walk into Borrowdale, but for me, as for many who know the Lakes, his sentence could be the district's epigraph. The prospect – and not only the view – changes continuously.

I was brought up a few miles to the north of it, and yet from the Lake District I drew the single most dominating feature in the landscape of my childhood: Skiddaw. An ancient broad slack-pelted fell, it beckoned and brooded on the southern horizon and we must have looked at it a dozen times a day, for the weather, out of habit and possibly for luck. To me as a child 'The Lakes' were indeed a magic place, rarely visited but on those special occasions full of wonders – great boulders which stood poised to hurtle down cliff-sides, waterfalls that dropped sheer down glistening slate, and the Lakes themselves, oceans of imagination to us, then, as we swished across them on Edwardian pleasure boats. I would have believed without too much pause that Excalibur did indeed rise out of Bassenthwaite Lake from where Tennyson was inspired to conjure it.

Adolescence admitted me to the Youth Hostel Association and walking the length and breadth of the place. Hot summer slogs up Scafell, hours lost in mist on top of Hardknott, calm courting evenings in Patterdale, saturated days

SCAFELL PIKES FROM HARD KNOTT, CUMBRIA

in the Eastern Fells looking for a hostel that seemed to have disappeared back into the hills like the fabled Arthurian rocks in St John's. I went to university thinking I knew the district and feeling sophisticated because I had decided that Wordsworth was good.

During the next ten years I visited the Lakes only now and then but always, truly, felt almost winded with pleasure at the sight and smell of them. Instant waves of resolution – to find a local cottage, to find a local job – broke on the dread rocks of mortgage, ambition and the perilous gathering of metropolitan pleasures. But the place came south with me and figured more and more in my fiction, though, perhaps unsurprisingly since the novels I write aspire to authenticity, the action hovered about the edges of the Lakes. Only occasionally did the fiction penetrate into the massif central which is the rock core. Founded as it was on an early stratum of recollected imagination, it held true to that and circled the border. Even when I eventually bought a small cottage it was in the northernmost tip of the National Park; just in it by less than half a mile.

Once settled into a routine of regular visits, I began to discover the place a second time. Partly through books: W. G. Collingwood, Norman Nicholson, William Rollinson, and further back into the eighteenth century West, Hutchinson, Gilpin, besides the Wordsworths, Coleridge, de Quincy, Southey, Harriet Martineau, Ruskin, Canon Rawnsley – the Lake District must have provided as much literature as any comparable area in Europe. The chief discoveries, though, came from my own walking and from my desire to learn about the place, to sit down and find out about its geology, its history, its industries, legends and traditions. What I unearthed was the foundation which supported and reinforced my previous passionate response: that the Lake District is demonstrably extraordinary. That upsweep of exalted feelings is raised on layers of material contributions which have deeply sprung the place.

It is a geologist's Valhalla. In Rhoughton Ghyll, for instance, where the big belly of a Northern Fell has been slit open for the operation of mining, twenty-three different minerals can be found within a few score yards;

including silver. These fells were laid down about 600 million years ago, and their undeniable similarity to massive docile elephants gently round-backed asleep ought not to lull any climber or walker into an easy feeling of superiority: the Northern Fells claim victims year in, year out. Further south, in the volcanics of the Ordovician period, even more fatal accidents occur; where once volcanic ash spurted and lava poured, bare and jagged rock now provides the testing ground for the Hard Men with their ropes and jangling ironware. Just a few miles south again, yet another geological age accreted its foundation 350 million years ago; then there were times of desert, followed by great bucklings, until finally the ice came and carved the district into its present contour. The result of this multiple activity within a very small space is what observers over the last two centuries have described as a unique and intriguingly varied landscape. Climb any fellside and, as the elegiac Gray truly said, the prospect indeed changes every ten paces. The rombustuous weather, hurtling across the Atlantic, sweeping over Ireland and the Irish Sea to be tossed up by the hills, adds varying colour and swiftly altered skies to the slowly changing earthscape. Nothing is regular, nothing is symmetrical, nothing is still. The earth movements go on, and it is as if the apparent antique settlement of the land is being constantly undermined by a subterranean restlessness — like coral reefs of minerals — which matches the often violent variability of the skies.

After the ice, the landscape was man-made. Over the years the greatest change has been the cutting of the forests; begun about 5000 BC by Neolithic man with his stone axe, the 'progress' of man in this district has been vitally linked to the destruction of trees. Even so, in the Middle Ages the greatest forest in the land was here, and the slaughter of 400 deer in a day by the King and his courtiers was not an uncommon event. But the Germans who came to open up the copper and lead mines at the end of the sixteenth century used so much wood that they were forced to dig for coal. Wars, charcoal burners and the steady demand for domestic fuel did the rest. The Fells are bare. Their nakedness is now emphasized — or is it embarrassed? — by the odd little fig leaf of reafforested conifers. The pelt smoothness has a rock-hard grandeur which

---

WASTWATER

ANGLETARN PIKES FROM ANGLE TARN

is deeply attractive to many of those who regularly come here. To them the mineral-speckled rock cropping out of the bracken, the bare hillsides which crest and furl like great frozen waves, the ingenious rivulations of the valleys unimpeded by deciduous bushiness are the characteristics that they most love about the place.

Like anywhere else, though perhaps here more evident, there are layers of settlement which make the landscape the open air textbook of a lengthy historical adventure. The most picaresque remains are the mysterious stone circles – notably at Castlerigg and Salkeld – still undecoded; there are Iron Age settlements high on the Fells, a reminder, among other things, that once this place was warmer and calmer; Roman remains – one spectacular 'enchanted fortress in the air' sitting side-saddle high on Hardknott Pass; the great Bewcastle and Gosforth crosses; Norman abbeys (most striking is Furness Abbey in Barrow, its sandstone glowing in the sunset); castles ringing the central mountains, guarding exits and entrances but by their very distance from the heart of the place lending credibility to the notion that the heart of the place was never conquered by the French – just as it was merely occupied, never crushed by the Romans. The sweep of building continued until its peak in the sixteenth and seventeenth centuries which brought to the district those enviable, secure, stone-built farm houses which seem planted on the hillsides or as inevitable in a valley bottom as the river bed itself. And finally the gentrification, happily in local materials: the subtly coloured grey and blue slates of Honister, Kirkby and Tilberthwaite and the Victorian baronial gothic clustered mainly around Bowness-on-Windermere are by no means an unpleasant addition. In short, then, as you walk the Fells – and it is as if the district had been designed for walking – you can rely on being enlivened by contact with the different intrusions of man. For just as it can still be a lonely place, so it has on that surface which is so dominating, enough well-defined and, generally, well-executed traces of previous encounters between men and the landscape to be a constant refreshment.

The heart of the Lakes is the hill farms, and it is the hill farmers, for me, who carry the real life of the district. Without them the land itself would soon

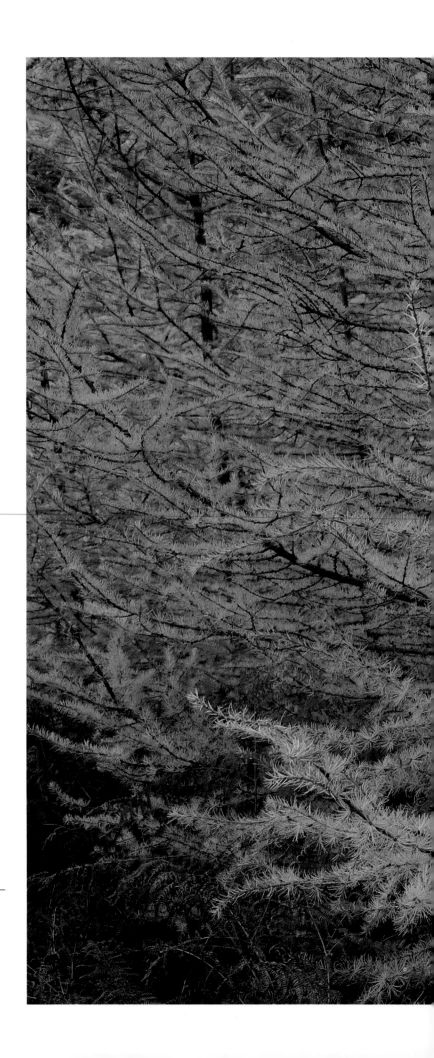

AUTUMN LARCHES, SMAITHWAITE BANKS

fatten and sprawl into unkempt parkland; without them the area would become no more than a natural playground. That it is still a place of work – and tough work – strengthens it profoundly: gives it that basic, functioning reality without which ski resorts and the like can seem to be mere toy-towns. The farmers maintain the dialect – almost wholly Norse and still miraculously surviving after nine centuries of opposition; they sustain the local sports – fell running, wrestling, hound trailing, foot hunting. It could be argued, romantically but with some supporting evidence, that deep in the heart of the district are still the descendants of those Brigantes unquelled by the Romans. They survived the Eagle Empire to graft on to the later Norsemen, who had adopted the Fells as their home and indeed gave them their name. That Norse–British splicing could well be the racial bedding of this land, as strong as the slate beneath the turf.

The power of the place though is not yet exhausted, for it was here that Western Europe discovered a laboratory of the mind in nature. The great passion for nature, that enormous change in appreciation and imagination which decided to turn to the once hostile, once barbaric, once despised and merely looted landscape as the place in which we could discover ourselves in the largest and deepest sense, executed much of its early drama here. Daniel Defoe, for instance, on his tour of the British Isles in the eighteenth century, sensed the new mood immediately. It was a perilous place, he reported, dangerous, a wilderness, horrendous; and, he implied, ripe to be tamed. He had written *Robinson Crusoe* in much the same vein: modern enlightened man was to go out to the wilderness in a spirit of conquest but would remain there only because of the power of his curiosity and the new conviction that nature had to be understood, to be treated as an associate – even, as time went on, a wiser, better, superior teacher.

Where Defoe led, the hacks and print-makers, the poets and scientific investigators of the landscape, the roving scholarly clergymen and the nomadic poets followed. The great and initially romantic movement to Naturalism had begun. In this Lakeland landscape was discovered material for speculaton on the origin of the planet – not in theology, but in geology – and

BUTTERMERE AND CRUMMOCK WATER FROM FLEETWITH PIKE

DEERGARTH HOW ISLAND, THIRLMERE

ESKDALE FROM HARD KNOTT

on the sensibility of humankind. Perhaps most influential of all, it was here that Wordsworth preached the healing force of nature and its appropriateness as a source of morality:

> One impulse from a vernal wood
> May teach you more of man,
> Of much evil and of good,
> Than all the sages can.

As the nineteenth century progressed, more and more disciplines and impulses found the Lakes to be an ideal testing ground – literally, indeed, in the case of those who, about a hundred years ago, invented the sport of rock climbing here. Landscape as a subject for painters overtook religion, mythological and historical subjects with astounding swiftness; the country and all things natural became increasingly revered as the main-spring of health, physical, mental, spiritual, even religious.

All these voices are still heard. As you walk across the Fells they filter through your mind, a mind already satiated with the subtlety and the splendours of this lovely and varied place. There is nowhere in my experience like it.

GRAINS GILL, SEATHWAITE

Recently constructed motorways have brought the beauty and the peace of the Lake District within one and a half hour's drive of thousands of Lancastrians and Yorkists and within weekend distance of many more Londoners. Consequently the area has now become one of the most heavily visited mountain playgrounds in Europe. This is creating problems which profoundly affect the wildlife and natural features it embraces. The first and most obvious problem is feet.

The small National Trust property of Tarn Hows, for example, can receive 250 vehicles at a time, bringing so many people to a confined space that there is real danger of their trampling it to destruction. For experiments have shown that if more than about 10,000 people walk over the same piece of turf in a year (and that is less than thirty a day) the surface will break, the soil will be exposed and erosion will follow. As the path becomes loose and muddy, walkers spread further over the terrain, widening the area of erosion. Even where the turf remains intact around the edges its character is altered: very few species tolerate continual trampling, and only plantains and daisies, with their leathery leaves which hug the ground, may survive.

In lowland Britain temporary exclusion of the public results in rapid natural regeneration of the sward, but on the thin, poor, wet soils of the mountains growth is slow. Regeneration may take several years, so firm decisions have to be taken either to close paths or to provide alternative routes.

Millions of visitors also, sadly, bring in their wake a litter problem. Not only does litter disfigure the landscape, it also pollutes and alters it. Plants of the open moor are replaced by nettles and docks and other species that flourish in 'well-fed' soils. This process is aggravated in the absence of toilets, but even where these are provided they only transfer the problem to the lakes: water so enriched increases algal growth which blankets and kills many submerged flowering plants.

Even on remoter crags the weight of numbers is destructive. Sheer cliffs are a challenge to climbers ever keen to seek new routes rather than queue for those already over-subscribed. The climbers inevitably disturb nesting birds such as peregrines and ravens, and if they do not themselves uproot rare alpine plants they may open the way for collectors to reach the previously inaccessible.

These same crags attract scores of geologists, and many of their fine rock exposures are literally taking a hammering as collectors search for fossil starfish and brachiopods.

With pressures on such a scale conservation organizations, many of which have among their objectives education and enjoyment, are faced with a problem. How can they continue to keep their reserves open when the visitors are destroying the very treasures which the reserves were created to protect? Yet how can they put up 'Private – keep out' notices without turning against them the public whose support they need if they are to protect endangered sites? This dilemma must be resolved, but nowhere in Britain is it more pressing than in the Lakes.

HONISTER PASS

THE
HIGHLANDS

IAIN CRICHTON SMITH

The Mountain

In summer the deer are questionmarks on the mountains
feeding among the cress.
Their antlers burn in the sunrise.

I have drunk water so sweet
that it was the wine of the wind
brewed in quiet hollows.

We have climbed to where the eagle turns
negligently towards a cloud
with its freight of meat,
and awkward among scree we have slithered
from peak to peak.

I have felt your sweet bones, mountains,
like the bones of a cat,
and sometimes in an autumn evening
the untethered moon drifts.

126   STOB DEARG FROM THE RIVER COUPALL, STRATHCLYDE

In winter you are white maps,
ice triangles.
The birds and herbs have been squeezed out of
your chained kingdom
where the rivers are quiet
and your skin is an amazing
naturalized ghost.

The green forgets itself.
There is a symmetry
of cruel perfection,
aristocratic, brutal,
an upthrust of eternal
peremptory music.

Startled, we gaze
into the kingdom of the dead,
these peaks of absence
where all has been changed to silence
and the chimes cannot be heard
of these congruent crests.

Argyll

Rowan trees, birches, roses, and calm lochs,
to you Columba came,
imperialist of the spirit, with his books.
This is a rich land, not monkish,
a theatre of the wild.

THE RIVER AFFRIC, GLEN AFFRIC, HIGHLAND

LOCHAN AN DAIM, TAYSIDE

LOCHAN NA H-ACHLAISE, RANNOCH MOOR, STRATHCLYDE

STOB NAN CABER, GLEN COE, HIGHLAND

The buzzard rests on the wire, the rabbit
marries the stoat's ring,
and on the hills with their fine scholarly heads
I see my elegant deer.
The wise salmon slides downstream.
The fox burns in the frost.
The trees create a technicolour autumn
in orange and in gold.

Glencoe, you are I think the only weeper
for that winter massacre
assassination on the frozen lochs,
the quick jab of the knife.
But otherwise the rowan berries shine,
an astronomy of wounds,
and waters reflect hills exactly
in their mild immobile glass.
The pheasant like a stained-glass window stalks
proudly among your fields,
illuminated missal, rainbow bird.
And in the Holy Loch the missiles sleep
like rows of organ pipes.

After my bleak island I adore
the largesse of your fruit,
the bramble berries mapping gloveless hands,
the ballet of your birch,
the sea that shines to Islay and Tiree,
to Iona and to Coll.

Such jewellery you have, my calm Argyll,
mild dowager of tales.

You might think, pausing as you climb to look at the peaks all round you, with not another being in sight, that the Highlands remain the last great wilderness in Britain. But it is an illusion, for they are already in the process of being destroyed.

Those native red deer silhouetted majestically against the skyline have spent most of the day in the small remnant of deciduous woodland which follows the course of the burn, browsing on saplings which will never become trees, and condemning the wood to a lingering death.

Now the herd, too large for the land left after afforestation has fenced off the lower ground, is grazing and trampling a steep grass and heather slope, breaking the surface of the sward. In winter, water will penetrate and turn to ice, heaving earth to the surface which will be washed away in the spring rains. Gradually the whole slope will lose its cover, and acres of bare scree will join the others which already scar the landscape. Uncontrolled deer are an ecological disaster.

The solitary silence is shattered by the high whine of a Land Rover following the route of a brash new road which jars the rounded contours and leads to an unmajestic metal mast conveying TV pictures of unspoilt landscapes to isolated crofters. Where one rover leads others follow, illegally on wheels or legally on foot, disturbing the wildlife.

Some summits are too steep for roads but thought fit for skis. On the far side of that mountain to the north a chair-lift is being erected. In winter thousands of Coke-can carriers will line its crest before plunging downwards – too often on snow so thin that the fragile turf is further damaged. In summer more chairpersons are lifted aloft to wander and trample, bringing dangers to rare species once protected by their remoteness.

The dying woodland, eroded slopes, ugly roads, obtrusive masts and litter are obvious to the seeing eye but other, hidden forces which are equally damaging are at work all round.

There are no eagles now riding the wind above the crag which once concealed their eyrie. They have been poisoned by shepherds who wrongly supposed they lifted living lambs when all they took was carrion. Peregrine populations, recovering elsewhere after the ban on organochlorine pesticides as sheep-dips, have not risen here. At night the egg-collectors have used the new road for a quick trip to rob their nest.

There are no living trout in the burn below, for acid rain has been falling, releasing into the water toxic aluminium which attacks the gills of the fish, leaving them to die from lack of oxygen.

The return from the wilderness is now much quicker than it was: spurred on by subsidies from public funds, farmers and foresters are taming the lower slopes, ploughing, reseeding and planting, and thus destroying the moorland.

While you paused the wilderness diminished. If we do not rouse ourselves to combat the dangers, the wildness and the wildlife will disappear as swiftly as those deer which have now slipped silently over the brow.

LOCH LURGAINN AND STAC POLLAIDH, HIGHLAND

ORKNEY

GEORGE MACKAY BROWN

It is best perhaps to come to the islands in midsummer; then the late-setting sun dips under the north-west horizon only briefly, to rise a few hours later in the north-east. The sun-glow never leaves the north.

In that glimmering enchanted twilight the farms lie sleeping in valleys and along the sea shore. The fields with their increasing burden of ripeness, and the animals, lie with the blessing of dew on them. The tilth lands and pasture seem timeless, as if they were from everlasting to everlasting. The quiet skies, waters, hills, have the quality of ancient heraldry.

It is a people contented and at peace. You can tell that from the slow unhurried lilt of the country speech.

It was not always that way.

Many small wars, raids and plunderings and stormings, went to create that peace.

Summertime Orkney is not the whole truth. Come in midwinter, and taste another kind of magic – the dark storms that fling spindrift higher than the crags and lace with stinging salt the links. The great tempest of January 1952 blew henhouses out to sea, cockerels raging aloft. The long winter darkness has a different heraldry: stars, the changing orb of the moon, occasionally (between gales) the beautiful dance of the aurora borealis in the north.

BAY OF HOUTON, MAINLAND, ORKNEY

CRAIG GATE FROM RACK WICK, HOY

Edwin Muir, himself the son of an Orkney farmer, but long a stranger to the islands, rediscovered them in his Scottish journey in the mid-1930s. Orkney seemed to him then the most prosperous and contented community in a Scotland racked by economic and industrial stagnation. Childhood memories had provided him with the symbol of Eden that he uses with such luminous power in his verse.

Nothing much has changed in the fifty years since *Scottish Journey*. But it is impossible to appreciate the Orkney of today without the dimension of history. We are the mingled weave that many hands have worked on.

The feet of many strangers have visited the islands in the course of six thousand years or so, and have stayed, compelled by a magic that is still operant. (Orkney has two opposed effects on strangers; either it attracts them strongly, or else they take one appalled look and turn away.)

What human foot first touched a shore here, after the slow retreat of the ice, no one can now say. In the island of Papay has been recently unearthed the oldest dwelling-house in Europe. It is strange to think of those remote ancestors drinking the same wind, measuring with eye and oar the same tides as ourselves. What their thoughts and speech were, no one will ever know. The harshness of their circumstance meant that they probably did not live long; a man was old when he was in his thirties. They were delicate and marked for an early death. But what amazing courage, to set out from the north coast or the west coast of Scotland, to the islands that lay further north still, dark and glimmering on the water like sleeping whales. For their boats were as light and delicate as themselves, and the sleeve of sea they had to cross was the Pentland Firth, one of the world's wildest sea-passages. Not only themselves had to embark, but the livestock on which they depended had to be laid, bound and bolt-eyed, in the ships. So they stepped ashore, on Hoy or on Ronaldsay; and the skippers eyed with dismay the weave of heather and fern everywhere. But the poet of the tribe put beauty of harp and voice on the new place, a beseechment or a coercion. Within that poem of increase we still perhaps live, though the words of the chant are lost.

SEAWEED, WAULKMILL BAY, MAINLAND

The poem of greeting and welcome first, then the settlement, the clearing of land for the plough (if those early ones had knowledge of agriculture at all), the probing of the sea for fish, the building of a larger house for the chief than for the others (stone it had to be, for the place had few trees). Nor did they neglect to build a chamber of death for those who died that first winter: the very old and the very young, and the girl who, racked with seasickness on the terrible crossing, never got her strength back.

'Brief, brutish, and nasty' perhaps: but through the wretched weave runs the red thread of courage.

The poet sang silver elegies at the end of that first winter.

The whole story of the islands is a repetition, with variations, of that first coming.

Those discoverers were not suffered to dwell unmolested in their valley, or on the margin of their bay, where the soil was sweetened with blown shell-sand. The same urge that had driven them to break the horizon northwards brought sequent tribes, possibly of the same basic stock as themselves – then the shore stones were splashed with blood, the caves echoed with rage and defiance.

Invasion, uprooting again and again and again: until at last a skilled ruthless people established themselves; and probably their old chief was in his forties (so much higher the cornstalk grew). And at his long table the harvested corn, changed to bread and ale, was broken in peace. *They* would not easily be chased from their acres. But what is a hundred years, or even three centuries, in the eye of time? Other stronger north-farers took over the fields and the fishing boats, the stones of the township too were reddened. A new chamber of death was opened, with reverence, to receive the wounds and the stillness.

And another poet harped and cried over the conquered glebe.

These are but conjectures, pictures of the past in a twentieth-century imagination.

There came to Orkney a people who had curiosity about the movement of sun and stars and planets, to whom the winter night-skies were a perpetual wonderment. At Brodgar, between the two lochs, they sought to capture the subtle movements of the stars in a stone web. The stones of divination are still there, in a wide circle, a few of them broken down and eroded by centuries of lightning, storms, rain. The stones at Brodgar may have been fertility symbols, to ensure ripeness of corn and of animals. They might – so daring and ingenious those people – have symbolized a first groping towards the mysteries of time and eternity; for a circle has no beginning and no end.

Near the two stone henges of Stenness and Brodgar lies the most magnificent stone-built burial chamber of all: Maeshowe. It was as if all the little honeycombs of death built by the earlier tribes had in Maeshowe their majestic consummation. Death, the end of all things living? The poet-architects of Maeshowe had so arranged their chamber that the midwinter sun, as it sets over the Coolag hill of Hoy, sends a fleeting beam through the long corridor and makes a splash of gold on the opposite wall. It is seen, that marvellous symbol, only on the few afternoons clustered about the dark solstice.

There came a people, possibly early Celts, and took possession of the islands; they built primitive stone keeps, or castles, along the shores and beside the lochs. Those brochs were marvellous edifices against the weaponry of the time. They were not built for fun; the sea-borne tribes were still moving west and north, seeking, through violence, the cornstalk and the fish that were (on the long table) symbols of peace at last. But now the Orkneymen knew how to defend themselves. The whole township, in times of trouble, was closed inside the impregnable broch, each with its animals and children. They endured, between the fire and the well of sweet water, until the besiegers got disheartened and sailed away, a few with bruises and burn marks on them, and the mocking satire of the Aikerness poet echoing still in their ears.

The old chief – who might now, near death, be in his early fifties (higher still grew the cornstalk), herded the people out to their unconquered fields and shores.

HOY FROM MAINLAND

SKIPI GEO, MAINLAND

PEAT HEATH, QUEEFIGLAMO

The Picts came, and left a few enigmatic stone carvings, and ploughed out more bog and heather . . .

Now the Orkneymen expected invasion to come always from Scotland or the Hebrides; only from those airts the perennial danger.

The Norsemen broke into Orkney from the east – first as pirates and raiders, but at last as settlers, for they could see well enough how the land had been tamed and made fertile by the plough and the ox, the sun and the rain and the seed.

They were so contemptuous of the settled Picts that they did not even bother to mention them in *The Orkneyinga Saga,* that marvellous record of the history of Orkney over three centuries. In no time these blond warriors in their beautiful dragon-headed ships possessed the islands utterly. A line of magnificent Viking earls ruled Orkney and Shetland. There was Earl Sigurd, who led his Orkneymen to the Battle of Clontarf in Ireland, in 1014, under the death-bringing, victory-bringing raven banner woven by his mother; Earl Thorfinn the Mighty – Macbeth's kinsman – who ruled nine earldoms in Scotland and was more powerful than the King of Scotland himself; the two joint earls, Hakon and Magnus, whose intersecting graphs came together and were sealed in blood in the island of Egilsay, and who fared forth again, Hakon to a peaceful and plenteous rule over a contented folk, and the soul of the martyred St Magnus 'to the fair pastures of heaven' (the great cathedral of St Magnus still stands, where many miracles of healing took place); the most attractive character in the Saga, Earl Rognvald – chevalier, poet, pilgrim to Jerusalem, 'master of nine crafts', whose golden days were ended by violence at a farm in Caithness; and the lesser earls, with whom the story peters out.

A brave tapestry they wove, the Norse Orkneymen.

Then came the Scots as rulers, administrators, taxmen; and it was 'the end of an old song'. The nine earldoms shrank to an unimportant group of Scottish islands, fair game for the plucking.

So Orkney entered a dark age lasting many centuries, with only a gleam here and there.

RING OF BRODGAR, MAINLAND

Our near ancestors endured a long age of oppression and misrule. The dark stubborn earth they worked was grained into them – sea salt was in their veins. They endured, and now their great-grandchildren move and work in quieter times and reap a moderate prosperity (it is no unusual thing for Orkney men and women to live into their eighties and nineties: so much time the tall oats and barley yielded them).

The medieval village of Kirkwall grew beside St Magnus Cathedral. Today it is the capital city – the prosperous mercantile and administrative heart of Orkney. The only other town, Stromness, is wedded to the sea. Adventurers and skippers move through its briefer history, all salt yarns and gulls and tar.

There are a handful of villages in this island and that, with shop and kirk and pub.

But still the real Orkney is to be found in the farm-steadings and houses 'sunk deep in time', with the heraldries of corn and beast, and the Atlantic fish . . . All around, the brown and green hills rise and fall like waves.

How much longer?

No community stands still. Today is a kind of small golden age for Orkney, without heroes or saints (who tend to show themselves only in times of peril and distress).

Oil has been found in the North Sea off Orkney; but the terminal and tanks and ships are confined to one island in Scapa Flow: Flotta.

It is known for a certainty that the soil of Orkney is moderately rich with uranium ore. The Orcadians – people slow to enthusiasm or indignation – closed ranks a few years ago when there was a move to make probes under their acres.

Earth-gold, sea-silver: these have been the signs on our heraldic shield, for many centuries now.

The islands have never been slow to welcome new things – field enclosures, machines, piped water, electricity – once they have convinced themselves that the innovations will lighten their yoke.

But from this element that has been waiting under their furrows from the

OLD AND NEW HEATHER, ORPHIR, MAINLAND

LOCH OF STENNESS, MAINLAND

beginning, they turn away, they have nothing to say about it, they feel it to be more alien and dangerous than the first bronze axe laid on the stones of Skarabrae. Concerning uranium, the poets and artists are silent, or they put a warning finger to their lips. (How could there ever be an ode to uranium?)

But nowadays the voice of art is drained of its ancient power, as we leave the age of the word and are gathered – whether we like it or not – into a bleak grey time when 'the number' will compel our goings and comings, and the good heraldry over our doors is a blank.

There was a time when fluctuations in the population of plants and animals on our shores and in the seas around us were controlled by storms and tides, exceptional frosts or prolonged droughts, and our modest harvesting of fish, fowl or laver-bread had only local, short-term effects. But all that changed with the growth of the oil industry. The transport of millions of tons of a poisonous and buoyant liquid in vulnerable vessels of ever increasing size across oceans and through congested coastal waters to terminals in enclosed harbours, has produced a threat to the wildlife of the four-fifths of our globe which are seas and oceans and all the coasts which border them.

This threat is intensified when the origin of the oil is the sea-bed itself and the wells and terminals are closely congregated, as around the northern isles of Orkney and Shetland. The threat became a reality at Christmas 1978 when fuel oil spilt from the *Esso Bernicia* in Sullom Voe, Shetland, killing at least a dozen otters and injuring many more, and oiling thousands of sea birds, especially awks such as guillemots and razorbills, the majority condemned to a lingering death.

Oil damages the plumage of sea birds, allowing water to penetrate the air spaces between the feathers and skin so that they lose buoyancy and sink. Even if they do not drown, the removal of an insulating layer of air causes such a rapid loss of heat that they soon exhaust their body reserves. With their natural food also polluted they die of starvation, a death accelerated by the toxic effects of ingested oil which damages their liver and kidneys as they try to clean their feathers by preening. The most sophisticated bird rescue centres can do little to clean and rehabilitate badly oiled birds in large numbers, and the only humane act is to destroy them.

Many techniques have been tried to limit damage by oil pollution. Some physical methods in the open sea or on sandy beaches are effective but the chemicals used, especially in confined spaces, have often caused more harm than the oil itself. Coasts such as rocky shores and saltmarshes are almost impossible to clean up: the effect of an oil spill may last for decades.

The best solution to oil pollution is prevention. An obvious and necessary move is the installation of sophisticated navigational aids and electronic devices in tankers to reduce the chance of accidents. Recent figures show however that the largest part of pollution by tankers does not arise from collisions but from the way they are operated – for example, the washing out of tanks at sea. With satellite surveillance of the world it should surely soon be possible for unlawful pollution by tankers to be recorded and reported so that the guilty can be punished by an international court. Clean seas are vital to the future of marine wildlife, and only determined action on an international scale can prevent further destruction of their living resources.

THE OLD MAN OF HOY